ON THE ROAD
A journey through a season

Daniel Harris

A Speakeasy Books paperback

Published by Speakeasy Books, 8-9 Pratt Mews,
London NW1 0AD

ISBN 978-0-9565944-0-2

www.speakeasybooks.co.uk

www.danielharriswriter.co.uk

Design by Diane Hill
diane@djhill-creative.co.uk

Printed in Great Britain by the MPG Books Group, Bodmin and King's Lynn

Acknowledgements

Thanks to John Brewin at ESPN Soccernet for asking me to write for him and for giving me the space to talk pretty much any rubbish I fancied. Thanks to all those who've read said rubbish in draft form and been happy to blacken their reputations by endorsing it – I'm very grateful – and in particular to Richard Kurt for his sagely cutting advice. Thanks to Benjamin Field for sending me things I'd missed, and for the occasional use of his secretary and trainee, and thanks to all those who in one way or another were generous with their help. Thanks to Samuel for the website and Gumbo for the photo. Thanks to Mum and Dad for their love, and thanks to the late Eric Harris for his love of United. And thanks to Belinda for everything.

Foreword by Michael Crick

The 2009/10 season could well mark an important turning-point in the long history of Manchester United. And I suspect that many other United fans share my fears, but also my hopes.

It marked the 21st successive season in which United have either won a major trophy, or come pretty close. Since 1990, Sir Alex Ferguson's successive sides have stacked up an incredible haul of eleven championship titles, five FA Cup wins, four League Cup victories, and three European honours. Twenty-three trophies in 21 years - an average of more than one a season.

These two decades of unrelenting success are without parallel in the history of English football. Not even Liverpool in their prime kept up the success for so long.

In 2009/10, like many campaigns over the last 21 years we were fighting for three major honours right into the closing weeks of the season. In the end we finished with just the League Cup, and eventually stumbled in the closing stages of both the League and in the European Cup. Ferguson's gamble of lasting a whole season with just three established strikers finally went wrong, with serious injuries to first Michael Owen and then Wayne Rooney.

That gamble by Sir Alex was, in turn, almost certainly forced upon him by the growing debt crisis at Old Trafford. Although United took £80 million from the sale of Ronaldo to Real Madrid in the summer of 2009, Sir Alex failed to use the money to replace him with a top-class goal-scorer. He claimed the right players were never available, and the prices too high, but a year later those excuses look pretty feeble. And it's starting to look like the £80 million from Ronaldo will never be spent on new talent, as we were promised. Instead it will go towards paying the Glazers massive debts and interest payments.

United may be the best-supported club by far in British football, and the team may generate huge annual profits, but it can only be a matter of time before the Glazer family's huge indebtedness, exposed in great detail by BBC Panorama in June 2010, come to cripple the playing operation in much more serious ways than we saw last season.

But as Daniel Harris explains, in this witty match-by-match chronicle of the 2009-10 season, it was also a year of great hope, not just for United fans, but for football supporters in general. It was the year when United supporters rose in the tens of thousands in protest at the Glazer regime, and its constant draining of our club's resources - the year we started to make a difference.

Never before has Old Trafford seen such a powerful fans' movement. When I helped organise the Shareholders United Against Murdoch (SUAM) campaign back in 1998, we had barely a thousand people backing us, and the independent supporters association, IMUSA, had only a few thousand more. As we fought the proposed takeover by BSkyB through the winter of 1998/99, many United fans were vehemently opposed to SUAM's efforts. Most Reds, frankly, just ignored us, or were baffled as to why we cared about who owned the club. And so long as Ferguson kept winning trophies that indifference and apathy was pretty understandable.

But now SUAM's successor organisation, the Manchester United Supporters' Trust (MUST), is operating in a totally different atmosphere and on a completely different scale. In the space of just a few weeks it became a true mass movement among United fans. Never before has British football seen such a formidable protest movement at any one club.

However, success against the Glazer family won't come easily or overnight. The first bid from the wealthy Red Knights has been rebuffed, and they will have to rethink and regroup. And we ordinary fans must prepare for a long war of attrition.

That may well mean a lot less success on the pitch, as the Glazers try to raise more cash by selling players and cutting wages. From now on, we may have to get used to playing a lot less frequently in Europe, and to winning trophies a lot less regularly.

After 21 years of plenty at Old Trafford, may come a long period of relative famine. But if last season's green and gold movement holds its nerve then it will eventually succeed.

Above all, we MUST stay United.

Michael Crick,
June 2010

Contents

Contents

Pre-season 14/08/09

"Pain", wrote Naomi Wolf, "is real when you get other people to believe in it. If no one believes in it but you, your pain is madness or hysteria".

Although she wasn't talking about following a football club, she could have been; the pain must be real because others endure it too, but because each experience is unique, the madness and hysteria remain.

As a Manchester United supporter, some may think I'm a hypochondriac with no conception of what it is to suffer, but I can assure you I have and then some. Even if we discount a childhood blighted by Liverpool's pre-backpass law success, every present-day celebration is tainted with the sadness of absent friends.

After the 2005 Glazer takeover in that blackest of Mays – dire football, Cup Final defeat and European success for Liverpool (at least you can't win the league on penalties) – a significant number of time-served Reds were forced into proving that they really did mean it when they said that they weren't for sale.

For my part, there was no way I was paying off the debt of a family wanting to own the club but expecting the fans to buy it for them, though at the same time, I couldn't face a life without watching the shirts, so I joined a fairly large minority who go away from home only. Ok, there's still a 3% booking fee every time I buy a ticket, and I missed the first few games of the following season while I made my peace with that, but I'm now relatively comfortable with the compromise. And each time I think about going back, I remember that even in a previous incarnation as a City lawyer, I was unfamiliar with terms like rolled-up interest and pay-in-kind notes, on which I'm now a lay expert. Or maybe that's just why I'm no longer a City lawyer, but you get my point.

Still, seeing the takeovers of other clubs, I retain a large helping of pride in the resistance that was offered. Enough to defeat Murdoch in 1998, although it didn't work out second time around, at least we were savvy enough to realise we were being screwed and bothered enough to try doing something about it.

As it happens, I don't actually miss Old Trafford all that much. Don't get me wrong; I miss the things that surround the game, and every time I think about the fact that I don't go I feel like crying tears of vomit – but as far as the actual 90 minutes go, I'm less bothered. OT was already something of a theme park in 2005, and having wheedled my way in on freebies a few times since then, it's now a whole lot worse. Those who left at the time, along with those who've been priced out since, seem to have been uniformly replaced by people who learnt how to behave at a football match from either *Soccer AM* or Hyacinth Bucket.

But anyway, what of 2009/10? 18 titles certainly made for an enjoyable summer, but as the slog begins again I'm less confident than I've been for a while, with Ronaldo gone and the money we got for him sitting in the bank. Originally, I'd assumed that bank wasn't United's, but after chatting to someone who knows and whom I'm also inclined to believe, this probably isn't the case. I'm unsure, though, if this has made me more or less aggravated; with the team so patently in need of high-class reinforcements, not purchasing them is frustrating in the extreme.

What I am sure about, though, is that Michael Owen in a United shirt is equal parts eyesore and Eeyore, even if, looking on the bright side, you could argue that we've got rid of two unpleasantnesses and replaced them with one. On top of that, chances are he'll be a handy impact sub – although impact could also describe a first touch that reminds me of another overrated dwarf I was delighted to see join City's band of bribed mercenaries – and his propensity to injuries ought to ensure that Macheda and Welbeck get a proper go at establishing themselves.

The real problem, of course, is the midfield, though it oughtn't to be too much of an issue in the league. Whilst Ronaldo's ability to guarantee easy games against crap teams playing above themselves will be missed, the defence concede seldom enough and the attack score often enough to deal with pretty much everyone.

Europe, though, is different, United utterly outpassed by Barcelona in last season's final. It's fair to say that they were hampered by injuries and suspension, and slightly unfortunate not to go ahead before they scored, but notwithstanding those excuses – all legitimate in their way – it's impossible to argue that Barca weren't miles better than us, and everyone else for that matter. And despite all the fuss about their three up front, it was largely because in Xavi, Iniesta and Touré they had a midfield that kept possession so well their shoddy defence was rarely tested, at the same time as making sure that Messi, Eto'o and Henry got plenty of the ball.

To be confident about competing with them in an open game, some kind of box-to-box beast was required, along with a goalscoring schemer, and we've signed neither. Nonetheless, a 19th title could well still be filched; now that would deliver madness and hysteria of an entirely different order.

Birmingham home 16/08/09

Burnley away 19/08/09

Gleaming DeLorean at the ready, poised to drive into the future, Marty McFly receives some last-minute instruction from Doc Emmet Brown:

"When this baby hits 88 miles per hour... you'll see some serious shit".

Well, at Burnley on Wednesday night we saw United's future; less style and speed, but the shit is every bit as serious.

Walking towards Turf Moor, things didn't look promising. Hot, sunny, decidedly un-United weather, with bicep-hugging t-shirts and fashion-victim pedal-pushers to the fore. And when they suddenly become chic, things are very wrong. Though chic they were, set alongside replica shirts with "Owen" on them, worn both by adults who should know better and kids who rely on adults to know better for them.

Talking of which, I was faced with a similar conundrum once the game kicked off. The teenage lad standing next to me spent large parts of it texting his girlfriend, and it was tempting, in an older-brotherly kind of way, to point out that United will still be there for him when Harriet is long gone. But with the boys on the pitch not exactly backing me up I felt bad breaking the news, so reluctantly left him to his swt nthngs.

That aside, the usual clichés applied – attention-seeking mascot, stadium announcer blending kids' party entertainer with hip hop hype man, and loud music ruining the goal celebration. Turf Moor itself, though, is a decent place to watch football, if a little overpriced – which may account for the rows of unexpectedly empty seats. Stands close to the pitch, the low roof that does a good job of keeping the noise in also seems to stop it from travelling – the home contingent were surprisingly quiet, save for some noteworthily loud whistling before both half and full-time.

Anyway, well played Burnley, who looked pretty comfortable for almost the entire 90 minutes. From a United perspective, you'd hope that for them to beat us, they'd have to play at somewhere close to their maximum, but in the event that wasn't necessary.

For most Reds of my acquaintance, the last few days have confirmed what they thought they knew; all is not well. And, unlike the last couple of seasons, there's no confidence in the ability of the players and staff to rescue themselves after a slow start, despite how many times both have confounded us. Shorn of the get-out-of-jail-free card that was Ronaldo, if Rooney has a bad day, winning games will be a struggle.

Although the summer's transfer business is part of the reason for this, it's also the result of over-addressing one problem and thereby creating another. United's current incarnation played easily its best football in 2006/07. A younger Paul Scholes was one factor, a fit Louis Saha another, but so too was the threadbare squad; with the first eleven picking itself and those in it significantly better than any potential replacements, consistency of selection was enforced, allowing the team to gather rhythm and hone the devastating combination play that destroyed even the most disciplined of defences.

Of course the quid pro quo was that come the end of the season, the key men were knackered, United limping over the line in the league and ultimately hammered by a not necessarily superior Milan side in the European Cup semi-final, so Fergie went to work beefing up the squad. This allowed him to change rafts of players from game to game without significantly weakening the team, and even if it didn't work, the defence and Ronaldo could be relied upon to do enough. The result was two more titles, a European Cup, another final appearance, and a World Club Cup.

But with Ronaldo gone, the squad suddenly looks flabby, full of good players, but with very few of top quality who aren't defenders; arguably, Wayne Rooney is the only one. Berbatov could be another, but he's suffered from the system more than most. Initially forced to integrate without a pre-season, instead of allowing him to build a relationship with his teammates, he and those around him were swapped in and out, keeping them fresh for further disjointed play later on. Compare with Barcelona: admittedly aided by playing fewer games in a slower-paced league, but also committed to making as few changes as possible, creating a well-grooved unit able to extract the utmost from both individual and collective.

The palpable lack of attacking cohesion against Birmingham should have meant that the manager selected a similar team for Burnley, the players needing games, not a rest. Instead, five of the front six were rested, to predictably appalling avail, and no doubt the same will be so at Wigan on Saturday.

Unsure of his best eleven, Fergie seems equally ignorant of the best formation in which to deploy them. With a prosaic, pedestrian midfield, the onus ought to be on getting as many creative players as possible into the opposition half. 4–4–2 simply isn't the best way of achieving this, limiting the attacking capacity of those in the middle; 4–2–3–1 would do a much better job, with double the number of designated attackers and sufficient cover for the full-backs to get forward too.

What's also glaring is the need for a coach. Anderson and Nani are undoubted talents, with imagination that could enliven the drudgery, but all too often it verges on the fantastical. Though both are beginning their third seasons at United, neither is very much better than he was two years ago, and whilst they must take some responsibility, it's also a managerial failing.

For now, it looks as though this season will be 2002 without the good football, which at least will mean no championship medal and fewer win bonuses for Michael Owen. And if that's the silver lining, then we're talking about one big old cloud.

United 1 (Rooney 34) **v Birmingham 0**

United: Foster, Fábio, O'Shea, Evans (Brown 74), Evra, Valencia, Fletcher, Scholes, Nani (Giggs 46), Berbatov (Owen 74), Rooney. Unused subs: Kuszczak, de Laet, Gibson, Anderson.

Burnley 1 v United 0

United: Foster, O'Shea, Brown (Neville, 71), Evans, Evra, Park, Carrick, Giggs, Anderson (Valencia 59), Rooney, Owen (Berbatov 64). Unused subs: Kuszczak, de Laet, Gibson, Scholes.

Wigan away 22/08/09

On the way to the game, the chatter was whether we'd cede the points if it meant that the Glazers were forced to spend some money in what remains of the transfer window, the rationale being that not adding a bit more class in midfield would be more damaging than a defeat. In the event, the win amounted to more than a papering-over-the-cracks job, even if, to paraphrase *Pulp Fiction*'s Mr Wolf, there's no need for fellatio just yet.

Things didn't look especially great watching the players warm up. Usually it reminds you of how ridiculously good they are, and there were times when it was almost worth getting in the ground early to watch – particularly so in the days of Beckham and Verón, who'd stand the width of the pitch apart, and ping passes over the heads of everyone in between. However Saturday's shooting practice was amongst the very worst I've seen, and it didn't bode well for a successful afternoon. The man behind me had the right idea, leaning back in his seat, eyes clamped shut, and upon closer inspection he turned out to be someone regularly seen striking similar pose in various stadia across Europe, spawning his own parlour game, *Drunk, Narcoleptic or Blind.*

Anyway, back to the warm-up, there's this game United play, which I believe is called boxes. All the starting eleven, save the goalie, gather in a small square, and, divided into two teams, compete to retain possession of the ball. For the times when it runs out of play, there's a large cluster of replacements kept at one corner of the pitch; fair enough, no point them wasting their time chasing around. What's quite remarkable, though, is that there's someone whose job it is to stand adjacent to this cluster and roll the new ball to the nearest player when required, lest one of them have to move a couple of yards to get it for himself. That someone is also responsible for putting bench coats on those substituted, again to ensure against the expenditure of unnecessary effort; presumably he's handy with the loofah too.

United's team was again much changed from the previous game, but this time for the better, and with one or two exceptions was the strongest available. As ever, watching the huffing and puffing of Gary Neville was winceworthy in the extreme, but it was good to see Fletcher back. Handed the moniker of "The Scottish Player" early on in his career, over the last couple of seasons he's become the only automatic choice in midfield, and of everyone in the squad – in fact everyone in last season's squad too – has easily the highest number of outstanding big game performances.

Immediately after kick off, cute little Wigan manager Roberto Martinez began pacing the technical area, waving his arms with endearing enthusiasm to no apparent effect. Particularly noticeable was how far from fetching he looked in a suit so tan that even James Dean couldn't ensuaven it, teamed with a pair of broon shoes that from a distance made it appear as though he was stood there in bare feet like a madman.

It was as I typed this observation into my phone that I realised how utterly I've shafted myself. When you decide to be a writer, you also decide to accept certain hardships, one of which is to be perpetually at work. It's a bit like revision for an exam; it's never finished, and even when it is, it isn't. Before now, going to the game had been pretty much the only thing outside of that remit, allowing me to get on with thinking of nothing but it, until here I am – actually recording the attire of Wigan's manager, when I should be focused on enjoying the famous Man United. A sad day indeed.

While we're talking matters metrosexual, it would be remiss not to mention suntanning policeman Howard Webb strutting around in his tight top, part beefcake part lots of cake. To give him some credit, he obstructed the play only twice, and did a good job of missing Vidić's foolish hand-off of Rodallega, whose resultant gibbering anger was one of the more amusing episodes of the afternoon. He was abetted in this tantrum by the rotund Jason Scotland, actually larger than his namesake country and even less useful.

Despite the chuntering around me, the first half wasn't too bad, and easily United's most cohesive of the season so far. Having Berbatov as a focal point made a huge difference, and though they can play plenty better, there were two or three sublime moves with him at their centre that should have ended in goals. That they didn't was down to wayward finishing, rather than anything done by puberty-face Kirkland in the Wigan goal.

Talking of Wigan players, I bumped into Mario Melchiot a few years ago, helping some friends film the opening of London's Ruff Ryders store. Showing a few skills to the camera, he repeatedly advised "it's all about the poo-see, it's all about the poo-see". Surprised by such bluntness, even from a footballer, it was only much later I discovered that "poo-see" is Dutch for nutmeg.

At half-time, there was the usual raffle or whatever, the prizes putting *Blankety Blank* to shame. First place received the odd sum of £510, second a meal at Rigalettos restaurant in Wigan's "exclusive" west stand, third a bottle of "Uncle Joe's", whatever that is. At least I think that's what it was – it could just as well have been Uncle Joe himself. But this was actually a rare occasion on which it might have been worth buying a ticket, with so few people in the ground – recently renamed the DW Stadium by chairman Dave Whelan in a staggering act of shameless narcissism.

Although Rooney seemed to get most of the post-match plaudits, Berbatov was easily United's best player. Against Burnley, there were two tactics: get the ball to Rooney on the edge of the box and hope, or get it wide and hope that the resultant cross somehow evaded the 47 enormous defenders massed around the goalmouth. Suddenly, there was another way.

It's a while since a player has so split opinion, the snobbery of Berbaphile aesthetes such as myself winding up those ingrates irked with his languid style and vice-versa. Following his goal, a mate of mine in the latter category commented on the smug glances I was unwittingly shooting at him, and he was right – along with a fair few others, I've staked my reputation on the indolent Bulgar, and each time he does something beautiful I find it impossible not to beam with vindication.

Most pleasing of all, though, was the developing understanding between his rapier and the Rooneyian broadsword, though both were overshadowed by Owen's goal, which precipitated the highlight of the afternoon. After what was a very nice finish, there was warm applause as he attempted to fraternise, followed by a heartfelt chorus of "You Scouse Bastard".

But trust him to ruin it. *The Guardian* reported that after the game, he refused to talk to any media other than United's own television station. "You cane me, then you want an interview?" he apparently asked, before quickly striding off.

So how does he think his missing of easy chances and general ineptitude should be reported then? It's not ok that Fergie refuses to speak to this one and that one, but at least he's earned himself some slack. Owen, on the other hand, has not, and this particular display of self-obsessed whining illustrates exactly why no set of supporters has ever taken to him, though in the context it's odd that he wasn't more popular on Merseyside.

This Saturday, United are at home to Arsenal – a game that could really have been done without for another couple of weeks whilst discovering some momentum is attempted. Doubtless a way of sneaking Park into the team will be found – not really necessary now Ronaldo has gone, and putting almost all the attacking onus on the centre-forwards. I don't dislike Park, who can be worthy enough in the right company, but the team needs inspiration more than endless running around, and both Nani and Valencia deserve to keep their places.

What will be interesting to see is how Arsenal approach the game. Despite the reputation constructed for them by the London-based media as altruistic cavaliers, at Old Trafford they tend to be fairly cautious. But with United's defence depleted and their attack playing well, hopefully they'll have a proper go and it'll be a decent game.

Last word this week goes to Mark Hughes. As someone who once had a hamster called Sparky, his blueness is a particular sadness, and this latest nugget is a perfect encapsulation of how utterly he has been consumed by the delusion. Crowing about his acquisition of Joleon Lescott, he commented that the player "is arguably the best centre-half in the Premier League".

Yes, Mark, you could argue that, but likewise you could also argue that black is white, white is black and both are green. Ralph Waldo

Emerson once said that "money often costs too much", and with that in mind, perhaps it's time for a lie down.

Wigan 0 v United 5 (Rooney 56, Rooney 65, Berbatov 58, Owen 85, Nani 90+2)

United: Foster, Neville, Vidić, Evans (O'Shea 72), Evra, Valencia, Fletcher, Scholes (Gibson 72), Nani, Rooney (Owen 71), Berbatov. Unused subs: Kuszczak, Fábio, Giggs, Welbeck.

Arsenal home 29/08/09

Quite a few replies to my first blog criticised me for my decision to stop going to Old Trafford after the takeover, with this one being my favourite:

"Daniel, please stop using the word 'we' when discussing Man Utd. You lost that priviledge [sic] when you gave up your support for nothing more than an owner change. An owner who despite creating a massive debt (which they are paying off) has done nothing but give SAF free reign to do as he pleases and in doing so brought an s-load of trophies. Get over yourself and stop embarrassing 'us'. We don't miss your type."

Initially, I resisted the urge to reply in terse terms, but this past week I've got to chastising myself for my uncharacteristic reticence in illustrating why I'm right. Prompting this was the closing of a transfer window in which United have managed to collect an enormous sum of money and not address the weaknesses in the squad, despite a need so obvious it's spent the last three months in a fluorescent orange cheerleader outfit singing "I am a need and I am obvious" to the tune of *Glory Glory Man United*. Given that Tampa Bay Buccaneers also left a chunk of their allocated budget for the draft unspent, despite a roster requiring similar reinforcement, this was not at all surprising.

But this kind of anecdotal speculation didn't work last time, so let's put it away, along with the bleeding heart, butchered heritage sentimentalism that was equally unsuccessful, and try a drier way of making the point. Here are some figures to make Jerome Kerviel wince:

United is jointly owned by two companies. In the last financial year, one of these – Red Football Limited – lost around £26.5m! Now I'm not a frequent user of exclamation marks, but I think you'll agree that astonishing fact merits one, and here's another: Red Football is a wholly owned subsidiary of Red Football Joint Venture, whose accounts for 2008 show a deficit of £42.7m!

During that period, United won the league and the European Cup. Yes, despite enjoying their most successful season in a decade, the club lost money – lots of it. Essentially, most of what it makes, plus a load it doesn't make, goes to pay off the interest – not capital – on the debt incurred by the Glazers buying it in the first place. In a convenient quirk of the financial system that has served us so very well, they're permitted to borrow from the banks to acquire United, before using the assets of the club – gate receipts, player sales, telly money, merchandising, television rights and the rest – to pay them back.

But that isn't all. In 2013, the club will have to find £75m to pay off the debt, plus interest on the amount still outstanding, and £150m for the next three years after that, also plus interest, making the total amount of senior debt £575m. £425m of that is secured against the assets and undertakings of Manchester United Football Club, even though the loan was made to Red Football.

And still it gets worse; there are also some very cute pay-in-kind (PIK) notes, the compound interest on which rolls up in its tidy, rounded, lovable way, at 14.25%. These are carried by Red Football Joint Venture. As of last month, the total amount of debt attached to them is chilling at the £205m mark, and by maturity in August 2017, will have gently nosed its way up to a simply delectable £597m. Don't you just love Glazernomics?

Making the kind of money needed to service this debt is utterly unforeseeable, even if United were able to negotiate their own television deal, which would help a bit. But there's no way of persuading a majority of league members to ever acquiesce; breaking the collective sale agreement would further widen the gulf between the very top and the rest, though maybe they'd mind less if in exchange they got a competition with no relegation.

Examining the current agreement on legal grounds could, perhaps, circumvent the problem. Any serious challenge would have a decent chance of succeeding in the European court, which tends to frown on arrangements controlled by effective cartel. If this happened, the consequences for the game in England would be disastrous.

Alternatively, and if other clubs were amenable, United could leave the Premier League and join a pan-European super league. This would actually be a good idea if it comprised only champions and replaced the current Champions League format, but if instituted to replace domestic competition, would be, to borrow Will Self's phrase, the diarrhoea icing on the shit cake.

The only other hope the Glazers have to get out of the hole they and the banks have dug is that someone of quite unfeasible richness comes along and takes the hit of the debt, and I suppose I'd just about prefer United to be a toy rather than a pension. Otherwise, they'd best give Mickey Thomas a ring.

In the meantime, every conceivable revenue stream is maximised, every possible cut in expenditure made, which is a bit like me throwing a punch at Brock Lesnar. Transfer market parsimony aside, the most obvious example of this is in admission prices, which have increased by over 40% since the takeover. So along with those who left on principle, there's now an additional tranche who've been priced out, their match-going as past tense as Mr Praline's parrot; no longer is there a simple, single statistic by which to measure devotion to the cause.

Now, as kids, everyone was told to look after the pennies and the pounds would look after themselves, which may have worked in terms of cola bottle acquisition, but is less a truism when the pounds are denominated in hundreds of millions. Nonetheless, United are doing their best, leading to an arrangement with ticketing website Viagogo. Season ticket holders unable to attend a particular game are able to list their seats on the internet, and if a buyer's found, a portion of the initial cost is refunded. Although the brief has been bought back for below face value, it is then resold for significantly more than that, in a virtual environment that is effectively a footballing Hamsterdam.

In the week leading up to the Arsenal game, there were 14 pages of tickets available. Ok, it's early in the season, and it was Arsenal, not Liverpool or City, but that would still have been inconceivable until recently, and is a pretty good indication that the levee is beginning to break. Sign o' the times mess with your mind, baby.

The game itself was good and bad. Excluding Berbatov was cowardly, though no doubt when Fergie dropped the bombshell he pulled it out of the air on the tip of his toe and killed it stone dead in one fluid movement. His non-selection – at home, nearing top form, and with one of the opposing centre-backs unused to marking players as good as he and Rooney – makes you wonder if he'll ever be allowed to participate in any big games. Instead, the latter will be subjected to interminable afternoons flogged alone up-front like van Nistelrooy before him, losing his temper, his hair and his youth.

Talking of team selection, for the last few years, the private messageboard of *Redissue*, one of United's fanzines, has run a prediction league in which people attempt to guess Fergie's starting eleven for each game. So far this season, including the Charity Shield, there've been four rounds, and sixty competitors each time have yielded three correct entries between them – not one of which was for last week's game.

Reflecting on the match itself, although the first half wasn't great, it certainly wasn't the one-sided annihilation suggested by some. United crafted two decent chances – one at the beginning and one at the end – as well as three excellent situations, all of which were wasted by Giggs. Arsenal passed the ball better, but weren't exactly shimmering with menace; Arshavin looked the only player likely to create anything, and his goal was deserved, but for the quality of the strike rather than any mesmerising dominance until that point.

It was in the first few minutes of the second half that Arsenal really looked sharper. Passing the ball incisively for the only period in the game, United's trousers, though not fully pulled down, were certainly hovering around the knee. But credit where it's due – they didn't flinch, taking the opportunity to show off the size of their testicles and handing Arsenal a bout of stage fright.

Fergie, on the other hand, had a bad case of shrinkage. Rather than go for it after the equaliser, he went to bring on Park – acceptable in replacing the execrable Valencia, but not the attacking change needed to exploit the shift in momentum against notoriously flaky opposition. Talking of Valencia, it would be wrong not to mention how hunky he looked in his new shrinkfit shirt, sleeves tight, short, and moulded around the contours of his biceps. ¡Qué un hombre!

Anyway, before the change could be made, Diaby – who showed some interesting skills both before and after his ridiculous error – glanced in the decider. After that, even though United were dicey as riley defensively, Arsenal rarely threatened, which in a way indicates that the three points were merited – going to the team stronger at the crucial moments and good enough to retain the advantage. Of course not having Manuel in nets also helped, but Arsenal had their chance before he got involved. You come at the king, you best not miss.

That isn't to say all is rosy, because it isn't. Rooney, Evra and Fletcher are in outstanding form, Berbatov has played well when selected, and Nani's improving – funny what a run of games can do, eh Alex? But the rest of them have largely been making up the numbers.

Couple of other things I thought I'd mention. Despite Wenger's sour reaction to the defeat, I felt elements of sympathy for him twice last week. His sending off was, of course ridiculous, but I was confused by Keith Hackett's grovelling apology, stating that the officials should've taken into account how little time remained on the clock. The laws governing this element of the game must be similar to those in place for derby fixtures, tolerant of violent tackling provided it occurs in the opening few minutes.

With regard to the Eduardo controversy, there seems very little doubt that he dived. But for banning him to be fair, the basis on which players can be charged for deceiving the referee needs to be uniform and explicit. If there are no objective standards, then it's not reasonable for those that attract most publicity to be punished. Currently, it appears that if the referee sees the offence, it's a yellow card, but if he doesn't, it's effectively a double red, provided requisite media fuss ensued. If a player dives to win a free kick on the touchline, that doesn't count, nor do any of the other occasions players lie to the officials to gain an advantage by means other than diving, even though all are covered by the law as it stands. No doubt nothing will be done.

One last thing for now. Listening to 5 live the other day, I heard a snippet that the new owners of Southampton have stopped giving free match tickets to ex-players and managers. The presenter then went on to say that one of these, Lawrie McMenemy was unhappy with the situation, which I found pretty unedifying. Fine, he was once employed by the club and did a decent job, but who's to say he's done more for it than its supporters? If he doesn't have an official role (and even then...), then unless he's seriously skint, he should pay in like everyone else – plenty of whom have less money than he, and none of whom had the privilege of serving the club they love in a professional capacity. I'll bet the Glazers have taken note...

United 2 (Rooney pen 59, Diaby o.g. 64) **v Arsenal 1**

United: Foster, O'Shea, Vidić, Brown, Evra, Fletcher, Carrick, Giggs (Berbatov 86), Valencia (Park 63), Rooney, Nani.
Unused subs: Kuszczak, Neville, Scholes, Anderson, Owen.

International week 04/09/09

I'd wondered what I might say this week with no games taking place, but I should've known better – there's almost always something. This time, it was accusations from Fiorentina and Le Havre that United acted outside of the rules in attempting to sign their players.

There followed a characteristic piece of meaningless posturing from David Gill, threatening to sue the French club for having the temerity to "insult" United. A world in which that were illegal would be a very sad place indeed, though it would at least have saved me from the choruses of *Man United Are Short-sighted* that soundtracked my childhood.

Anyway, so far, so playground. And to underline quite what a trifling, piffling little matter this is, Gill went on to inform us that he's "very comfortable" with the situation. Borrowing his phrasing from Peter Mandelson, another renowned bundle of honesty, the formulation is typically used to reassure silly old us that there's no need to be alarmed by the utter state the country is in. In a few months, once things have further worsened, he'll presumably have progressed to feeling "extremely relaxed".

Back to the matter at hand, without more of the facts, there's no real point in speculating as to whom, if anyone, is in the right. It is, however, worth noting that when people have a legitimate cause of action, usually they just get on with it – especially when we're talking about the Glazers. Or perhaps it's all a cost-cutting ruse, seeking to provoke a ban on incoming transfers.

Other famous issuers of idle threats include Sam Allardyce and Harry Rednkapp; accused by the BBC of transfer impropriety, they have remained curiously silent after publicising their intention to sue for defamation. As king of direct action Marlo Stanfield would say, "either do it or don't".

If nothing else, we can thank the controversy for giving us the opportunity to be lectured in morality by Sepp Blatter, one of those rare jokes that will never cease to be hilarious. But amongst all the pontificating, no one has stopped to wonder what might be best for the players. It's hard to imagine that Cesc Fábregas, for example – who moved to England at 16 – would have been better served playing in Barcelona's youth and reserve teams than featuring regularly in Arsenal's first eleven. Similarly, Ronaldo came to England at 18, and that went alright too.

That's not to say there isn't something very distasteful about going round the world collecting kids like Mia Farrow on speed, and, without doubt, some sort of regulation is required. But it's also important to protect the right of young players to decide where they live and play, as it is not to preclude them from developing their games in the best possible environment. Otherwise, some will have to watch their contemporaries improve faster than they are able, purely as a result of being born in the right place.

One imperfect solution to the problem might be to stipulate a number of first team games that players aged, say, 16-19, have to play, meaning that clubs could only buy those they planned to use in the immediate future. That would still rob some of the chance to learn from top players, but the pay-off would be regular first-team football.

What might also help would be for players to be represented by lawyers, not agents – skilled in negotiating contracts and easily capable of widening their expertise to encompass this specific area. Paid a retainer not a percentage, they would have far less scope for the parasitic exploitation of someone else's ability, and are bound by a professional code to act in their clients' best interests – one that isn't often broken at the highest level.

On to Saturday's game at Spurs and, as last year, the away ticket allocation has been reduced on the order of Haringey Council, due to persistent standing. One might have thought that they'd other, more pressing issues to concern themselves with, but evidently not. Particularly unfair is that United remain the only club thus singled out, despite plenty of others – including Tottenham – having plenty of supporters who do likewise. I wonder if it would be the same were the game not a guaranteed sell-out.

Not that that's really the point; it's long since been proved to be more dangerous for lots of people to stand suddenly at moments of high excitement than for everyone to remain upright throughout.

Nevertheless, the FA are steadfast in an intransigence that I've never heard accompanied by reasoned, factual argument, nor from the mouth of someone who actually pays for tickets and sits outside of the directors' box.

Much as they'd hate to admit it, there's a lot the FA could learn from their German counterparts. Several Bundesliga grounds incorporate large, safe terraces – on which it's also possible to be delivered a beer – and the success of their league is no coincidence. Prices are low, attendances are high, atmospheres are excellent and the league is competitive. Doesn't that sound absolutely rubbish? I too see no rationale whatsoever for imitating such a set-up.

Looking forward to the football, the question bothering most United fans is the Evra-Lennon contest. Despite a running style that suggests he's about to trip over his arms at any moment, he's about the only player to regularly get the better of Mad Paddy. There's not much Fergie can do about it either, beyond picking Park to play in front of him – never something to get excited about. Where's Mark Chapman when you need him?

Couple of other things I wanted to mention. I was watching the Depor-Madrid game last week, and though I think I noticed this last season too, I now have a blog on which to draw attention to it. Anyway, as a result of playing in the same side as Mahamadou Diarra, the identically-surnamed Lassana has ignored the convention of adding his first initial to the back of his shirt, opting instead for the (probably self-awarded) nickname of "Lass".

Leaving aside the smugness of it all, is this a choice open to everyone, or are there rules? What happens when 362 players in the English leagues decide they want their kit to say Trigger? What if Park decides he wants Ji-Spot on his?

And finally, just space for a quick snigger at John Terry. As part of ITV's coverage of England and Croatia, the starting line-up was revealed via pre-recorded footage, in which each player selected introduces himself by name and position. Terry, it appears, doesn't play centre-back but captain, once again showcasing the humility that has made him such a hero.

Then, after the game, he revealed that he'd been spat at by visiting substitute Ivan Klasnic, drawing attention to it for no discernable reason other than to reflect his own heroic stoicism.

"Their No17 spat at me. It's not a nice reaction. He came on frustrated, but it's not nice at all. He's the first person who's ever spat at me in my career. It's disappointing to see, but let's not let it ruin a massive night".

Yes, John, without your little pep talk, everything would have been spoilt for everyone. Oh John, you are so big. So absolutely huge. You are just so strong and, well, just so super. That's why you're father of the year.

Spurs away 12/09/09

Beşiktaş away 15/09/09

Bob Dylan's song *Like A Rolling Stone* tells the story of a girl who once thought she was better than everyone else. Then, her fortunes changed and she was relegated to the bottom of the social ladder:

"Once upon a time, you dressed so fine, threw the bums a dime, in your prime...you used to laugh about everybody that was hangin' out, now you don't talk so loud, now you don't seem so proud, about having to be scrounging for your next meal. How does it feel?"

Although I can't speak for the girl, the narrator's sentiments can be transferred just as easily to United's away support. Once in a league of its own, its composition has now changed enough so that save an unrivalled canon of songs, it's almost indistinguishable from those it used to look haughtily down upon.

Take last weekend's game at Spurs for example. Dominating the concourse pre-match was a small group standing in a wide circle like they were at a Jewish wedding, those involved staring down their friends' camera phones in an "I'm making this atmosphere me" kind of pose. As has become customary, this was accompanied by the chucking of beer over those minding their own, along with express, irrelevant singing. Wes Brown may well be the hardest man in all the town (if his pals are on holiday), but that afternoon he wasn't even in the squad.

Three days later, and United are in Istanbul. Given the size of the city, the usual plan of avoiding everyone else going to the game was uncomplicated. But during half-time, a kerfuffle developed – one that had, apparently, been simmering all afternoon – ending with headbutts, punches and bleeding. Like the beer chucking, this too is not uncommon, which is why, in answer to Bob's question, it feels like karaoke night in the loony wing of a borstal on groundhog day.

That aside, it's been a pretty good week. As is my wont, by the time the Spurs game came around, I'd convinced myself of the inevitability of victory, before turning up at the ground to discover that rather than the usual one or two surprise selections there were several, in a team with as much discernable shape as Beth Ditto.

After a minute United were behind, but after a couple more, they were playing well enough to suggest that this would be temporary. Having spent the last two seasons performing badly and winning anyway, defeat in this context was entirely inconceivable.

Showing all the skill of a *Deal or No Deal* champion, Fergie somehow stumbled upon the correct balance between legs and guile in midfield, the quartet interchanging to devastating effect. Fletcher excelled in the wide role that bought him so much derision earlier in his career, and for the first time the headline "Anderson Scores" needn't be atop a tabloid kiss-and-tell.

Knitting them together were *bubbe* and *zeide*, Giggs and Scholes; the former so flush with mysteriously grown football brain that you wonder if he's got a pet mouse called Algernon, the latter drilling inside-out passes like Boris Becker's backhand and free to keep the play moving without Carrick under his feet.

With Rooney and Berbatov playing well individually and in combination too, Spurs were a tottering pass-drunk mess well before full-time, completely incapable of competing with United's zest and zip. Even after Scholes took a rest, they remained superior, Rooney mesmerising and brutalising an entire back four so severely that even Harry Redknapp couldn't find anyone to blame.

On to Beşiktaş, and it was quickly obvious that their fans are a lot better than their team. The entire ground spent much of the game standing, bouncing and jumping, with flares and flags augmenting other more general merriment – things that if done in England would result in sanctions of one kind or another.

Even without officious stewarding and policing, though, it'd be silly to think that this kind of throbbing fanaticism could be replicated. Turks are loud, unashamed and uninhibited – in a good way – and emotional reserve isn't seen as an ideal.

So whilst in Britain, people go to the football to behave in a way that's forbidden in most other contexts, in Turkey – and to a lesser degree in Italy, Spain and Greece – it's simply an extension of what's usual, and from a higher starting point. Politics and religion are the same; people in the UK participate, but with nothing like the zeal you see elsewhere.

British football is also hindered by the import accorded to looking good. In other countries – even those where the national character is more temperate, like Germany and Holland – supporters are happy to look silly dressed in identical polyester monstrosities. Not exactly aesthetic, but it's a leveller and a disguise, encouraging unhinged behaviour in much the same way as a fancy dress party.

Less said about the game the better, but a couple of notes: Valencia was once again mercy-subbed, Blundetto to Fergie's Soprano. Nani, meanwhile, kissed the badge when celebrating Scholes' goal, the only feasible explanation that he'd replaced the red devil with a photo of himself.

Talking of self-love masquerading as passion, United play City this weekend, and with Adebayor banned, there's extra pressure on Tévez to get fit. When he left, I accepted his scoring against us as an inevitable but small price to pay for shifting someone I never liked or rated, and I expect most Arsenal fans feel the same about Adebayor. Melding the touch of a T-Rex with the nous of a gnu, they are but two of the many decent but not outstanding players City attracted over the summer, rather like how Paul Daniels ensnared Debbie McGhee.

It'll actually be interesting to see what happens should Tévez play and score, after the reaction to Adebayor's celebration last week. To the untrained eye, it may have looked as though it was designed to wind up the Arsenal fans, but luckily Leslie Hughes was on hand to enlighten us all:

"We just have to understand that he is an emotional guy and he wanted to share the moment with the fans in the corner with whom he has a special affinity".

Of course we know this to be untrue because we can see the pictures, but ordinarily we'd also surmise that one game in front of said fans could hardly constitute "special affinity".

But this is City we're talking about, their proclivity to falling in hopeless love the second somebody notices them the stuff of legend. Whether it's Rodney Marsh, Francis Lee or friendly Dr Thaksin, football's equivalent of the ugly, spotty, fat kid with an enormous library of pornography simply cannot help himself, after years spent watching his handsome neighbour get it on with everything in sight.

It's hard, though, to see very much wrong with what Adebayor did. When players receive abuse, fans may be surprised to see it returned, but that doesn't accord them the right to moral outrage. No one expected Eric Cantona to beat up Matthew Simmons, but that doesn't mean Simmons had legitimate reason to feel aggrieved, nor that he didn't deserve what he got.

The same is so with Adebayor. He isn't responsible for the behaviour of others, and neither should he be. A few seasons ago, Robbie Fowler scored for City against United, running to the away fans and showing five fingers, representing the five European Cups he hasn't won. Even by his exulted standards, this was not a pretty sight, but there were no complaints; we'd been giving him stick for years, he got the chance to retort, and understandably, he took it. Our reward was the knowledge that we'd got to him.

On the other hand, the three-game ban the FA awarded Adebayor for the incident with van Persie is a joke. He stamped on his head! Even in the UFC, where the aim of the game is to deliver maximum pain at maximum speed, that's against the rules – and they're in bare feet, not studs. Hey McFly, anybody home?

This little episode also highlights the need to alter how suspensions work. Adebayor should have been sent off against Arsenal (twice, as it happens), but stayed on the pitch to score the decisive goal. Now, he's banned for City's game against one of Arsenal's rivals, effectively punishing them twice.

To remedy this, why not have players suspended for the next time the teams in question meet? There'd need to be provisions in place to deal with cases of transfer, promotion and relegation, but that'd

be easy enough, and would be far more fitting a comeuppance –
I'm sure Bob would approve.

Spurs 1 v United 3 (Giggs 25, Anderson 41, Rooney 78)

*United: Foster, O'Shea, Vidić, Ferdinand, Evra, Fletcher, Scholes,
Anderson (Nani 82), Giggs, Rooney, Berbatov (Carrick 62).
Unused subs: Kuszczak, Fábio, Evans, Valencia, Owen.
Sent off: Scholes.*

Beşiktaş 0 v United 1 (Scholes 77)

*United: Foster, Neville, Vidić, Evans, Evra, Scholes, Anderson, Nani,
Rooney (Owen 64). Unused subs: Kuszczak, Brown, Fábio, Gibson.*

city home 20/09/09

Wolves home 23/09/09

It's generally held that football means so much because it means so little, and 150 years ago, that might have been true. Now, though, we know that nothing means anything; instead, things acquire importance on the basis of how they make us feel. If one of them happens to be football, then, quite simply, it means so much because it means so much.

In the absence of intrinsic value, we rely instead on our ability to experience joy. Liberally sprinkling it as our instinct and intellect direct, the resultant sensory pleasure reminds us we're real in the most visceral way. That's why we love football, and that's why we love life.

This week, I've been particularly keen on both, after one of the most delicious finishes to a game I've ever seen, combining the match-winning goal, the last-minute goal and the immediate response goal into a single blissful maelstrom. When the fact that it was scored by Michael Owen is no more than a quirky detail adding to the overall hilarity of the situation, the moment must be truly special.

To the game itself, let's first of all dismiss the fantastical notion peddled in some sections of the press that it was City's coming-out party. They may have shaded what remained of the first half after being gifted a goal, and only lost in injury time, but so what? For 45 whole minutes, they were absolutely pummelled; it was as though a stable of sumo wrestlers were standing behind Shay Given's goal, their weight tilting the pitch so that gravity had no option but to take the ball inexorably in that direction. And particularly gratifying was Munich Hughes' utter inability to intercede, all the more noticeable juxtaposed against Fergie's uncharacteristically effective changes.

In the days before the game, the notion of not winning had occasionally occurred, but each time it did, I reminded myself of the following four words: Richards, Touré, Lescott, Bridge. No team with that fugazi of a defence will ever amount to anything, a fact that United – and Arsenal a week earlier – exposed for all to see. And behind them, the excellence of Given's reactions may have kept his team in the game, but unless Sheikh Mansour's billions can somehow sway Mother Nature to supply him with a few more inches, he'll remain nothing more than a good small goalkeeper.

Of course he's still a fair bit better than Ben Foster, hardly an imposing presence himself. Originally, I'd have been happy enough that he learn to keep goal on the job, his shot-stopping and teammates good enough to mask the occasional error. However two of that sort in a game of that sort, in addition to the one against Arsenal, suggest that he's not, and may never be ready.

Talking of errors, just as glaring were those made by Rio Ferdinand, "The World's Greatest Defender" (we know this to be the case because Pini Zahavi told us). It's hard to condemn him for stepping out of the way of Bellamy's shot for City's second goal; if I were as dashingly handsome, I too would gutlessly avert my head at the crucial moment to save my boyish good-uns from potential damage. Similarly, I can forgive his brainless self-indulgence in giving away possession to Petrov in the build-up to equaliser number three; what I can't abide is his failure to flatten Bellamy before he got anywhere near United's goal. Most ordinary folk would relish such a chance regardless of circumstance, and yet when Ferdinand was in a position not only to do so, but to do so as a hero, making not even a cursory effort is unforgivable.

And as a direct consequence of this behaviour, he infected the populace with momentary feelings of warmth towards Michael Owen. For those who haven't experienced this odd sensation, it's a bit like finding another man in bed with your wife, then having to shake him warmly by the penis when you discover that their liaison has somehow brought about world peace.

While we're here, we may as well remain on the subject of Bellamy, one half of the world's first all-hunchback strike force and precisely the sort of oik you're desperate to see in a laser blue shirt. Following his assault of a pitch-invading United fan, City assistant manager Mark Bowen claimed that he acted in self-defence. Fair enough, you might think, except for the fact that the man in question was held by four others, his limbs entirely restricted; he was about as threatening as the Black Knight.

So exactly what kind of attack did Bellamy apprehend? Perhaps he knew the man to be half man-half lizard, with a long and venomous tongue? Apparently not; according to Bowen, he was scared of being spat at.

As any fule kno, the standard defence against spitting is to step out of range. Bellamy, however, did the reverse, racing towards it with alacrity in order to initiate a conflict where otherwise there would have been none. In the first instance, the invader was nowhere near him; their paths crossed because Bellamy couldn't resist the opportunity to unload a few more portions of the bellicosity that has won him such widespread love and respect.

By allowing him to escape without sanction, the FA have set the standard of acceptable behaviour interestingly low. If I were a player, I'd be plotting all manner of terrible revenges against opposition fans daring to breathe the same air as me.

As it was with Chelsea under Mourinho, it seems that each City game – even those they win – will inevitably be followed by a week of recrimination and bitterness. This time round the sense of injustice has focused on the six minutes of injury time that according to all but the bluest of moonies were correctly added.

In the song *Life's A Bitch*, Nas, echoing Pink Floyd and Bob Marley before him, observed that time is "illmatic"; an immutable, unstoppable force to which man is irrevocably subservient. But in the context of a football match, the reverse is so, as time is in the exact control of the officials – or at least it's meant to be.

In 2005/06, United were eliminated in the group stages of the European Cup, a suitable punishment for their half-arsed rubbishness. But at the same time, I remember coming away from game after game feeling like I'd not really seen one, and the statistics showing the number of minutes for which the ball was in play supported this impression. By judiciously fouling, time wasting and feigning injury, the opposition were able to prevent them from building any kind of pressure or momentum, the match reduced to a series of short vignettes with no continuity or flow.

I certainly don't blame the other teams for this, and it's not necessarily the fault of the officials either; the problem lies with the laws they're supposed to enforce. Until they're rewritten to describe exactly how timekeeping should work and when the clock must stop, what constitutes 90 minutes will remain arbitrary.

So with regard to Sunday's game, the discussion of how much additional time should have been played misses the point. Rather, the question is whether "a minimum of four added minutes" is even close to adequate for a half in which there'd been four goals, three substitutions, one booking and numerous set pieces. To save you all the bother of checking, I'll tell you that it isn't.

To remedy this, instead of leaving how long a football match lasts to the absolute discretion of the referee, why not stop the watch every time the play does and display it in the stadium for all to see? Time wasting will immediately cease, fans get their money's worth, and everyone will know how long they have to get that winning goal; yes, City, both teams are permitted to score in injury time.

Finally, a quick goodbye to a true legend of the game. This week, European Cup runner-up Peter Kenyon left Chelsea, and I'm sure I speak for the entire planet when I say that we can but dream of a world populated solely by clones of this incredible man.

United 4 (Rooney 2, Fletcher 49, Fletcher 80, Owen 90+6) **v city 3**

United: Foster, O'Shea, Ferdinand, Vidić, Evra, Park (Valencia 62), Anderson (Carrick 90, Fletcher, Giggs, Berbatov (Owen 78), Rooney. Unused subs: Kuszczak, Neville, Evans, Nani.

United 1 (Welbeck 66) **v Wolves 0**

United: Kuszczak, Neville, Brown, Evans, Fábio, Carrick, Gibson, Nani, Owen (Valencia 69), Welbeck (King 81), Macheda (de Laet 31). Unused subs: Amos, Ferdinand, Eikrem, Tošić. Sent off: Fábio.

Stoke away 26/09/09

Wolfsburg home 30/09/09

Although The Britannia is meant to be "a difficult place to go" – particularly in the current financial climate – last Saturday turned out to be fairly relaxing afternoon in Stoke. Reputedly the noisiest ground in the country, pre-match it was hard to discern whether that's so for people telling us it's so, but it's certainly one of the better new stadia, with a remarkably high concentration of people able to combust into hilarious rage whenever a throw-in goes against them.

Even after 25 or so years of watching football, though, I'm yet to get what it is that makes home advantage any kind of deal. The pitch at Stoke is a whole yard shorter than Old Trafford in width and length, but what else is changed? Eleven men each side, two goals and a ball; the game's the game.

Players will argue that they're affected by the atmosphere, but I'm not having that. As an ex-City lawyer, I know exactly what it's like to do your job with a bunch of aggressive losers in your ear shouting how much they hate you, and though I may have wished they'd shut up, offering it as an excuse for my underperformance would be risible to say the least.

There's not really very much to say about the game itself. Picking Scholes to feed two wingers was a sensible way of getting round a packed midfield, but the wide men stymied the plan with delivery so bad it put the Post Office to shame. At the moment, Nani and Valencia are misfiring opposites, the former with all the confidence but no idea what to do, the latter with no confidence so doing nothing with his ideas.

Thank Eric for reinvented winger Ryan Giggs; if only his purple patch were also a hair replacement device. Brought on in a substitution sponsored by Hollywood Signs – who might perhaps stock such a piece – within fifteen minutes, the game was over.

But despite this latest run of form, Giggs will always be a conundrum who never quite met his Harvey Freeman. An indisputable great, a player who epitomises the youthful flair and aesthetic beauty that make United United, he's also the most frustrating I've ever known and loved.

The other very best players of my United-watching career – Robson, Keane, Cantona, Schmeichel, Scholes, van Nistelrooy, Ronaldo – were all far more consistent, and generally played with greater intensity when things were going badly. And each one, with the exception of Scholes, carried the team for significant periods of time – something Giggs has never done.

To an extent, he's a victim of his position; it's hard to dominate a game from the wing, and it's hard to play well if you're reliant on service, though others have managed. But the unarsed body language, the bottled one-on-one in the 2003 home derby (a personal grudge), and the 2004–6 vanishing act remain severe and genuine charges.

To borrow Fergie's phrase, pinched from Paddy Crerand, a discussion of his time in the shirt can leave you with blood as twisted as those who endured the horror of marking him on a good day; not so of the others with whom he shares the pantheon. Judging him by his own stratospheric standards, any honest evaluation of his career leaves you wondering why he hasn't been brilliant more often.

And yet he's still close to the very top category. At his best, he's still the best, and it's sad to think that one day there'll be a United without him.

Until then, we're obligated to appreciate him while we can, arguably the architect of an enjoyable few weeks that have seen the return of the inevitable goal; a sure sign of a team that's playing well. For the most part, the attacking play has been incisive and sharp, even if the finishing is still ropey as ever, and I'd go as far as to say the football is better now than at any point in the last two seasons Despite defending badly, starting slowly and falling behind, it's a while since I've felt in apprehension of defeat.

This week's game against Wolfsburg was one such example, when after they scored, it was obvious that both an equaliser and winner would eventually arrive. An entertaining 90 minutes of football with more than a few moments of high class, what a shame it wasn't enjoyed by a full house. The relevant governing bodies need to start fining clubs for unsold seats, which they should be giving away free to the local kids who can no longer afford to watch their team.

It's been bothering me for two years, but during the game I finally clocked that what Anderson reminds me of is a Weebl, only with a fatter arse. And though he could do with losing some weight, he's also adept at using it to his advantage, coming along nicely now he's playing regularly. With Carrick rehabilitating after his run away from the ball turn at Spurs, there's suddenly decent competition for the role alongside Fletcher, even if we've still got no clue who'll be playing from game to game.

Anyway, a few other things. During the cricket international between England and South Africa the other day, home captain Andrew Strauss denied permission for opposite number Graeme Smith to bat with a runner when he was suffering with cramp, something football would do well to learn from. Extra time is dull enough as it is, without the flow constantly hindered by cramping players who should've trained harder. Fine, stop the game for genuine injuries, but cramp is a punishment for inadequate conditioning, and should remain so, or we may as well pause the action every time someone gets a stitch.

Though I didn't intend to go back over old ground, as I was writing this, I heard that Emmanuel Adebayor had escaped a ban for his goal celebration against Arsenal. Fair enough, so he should. However it turns out that he was treated leniently because of "the extremely provocative nature of the abuse he received". Excuse me? What abuse was this then? We know it wasn't racist, else we'd have heard about it specifically, so what might it have been, and what about it made it worse than the usual? No reporter or television mic picked up on anything unacceptably nefarious, nor did any Arsenal fans I've asked who were there, so how has the FA managed to?

It seems to me that the media has, for its own ends, determined the stick he deservedly received to be particularly harsh, City have run with it, and the FA have bought it. Perhaps they'd be interested in this bridge I've got for sale...

Talking of bridges, Phil Brown took the Hull squad on a walk across the Humber this week, where they came across a woman about to commit suicide. Apparently, Brown talked her down – this appears to be something of an expertise – and it's certainly easy to see how he was able to persuade her that things could be much worse.

And finally, after the roaring success of his insightful punditry and inspirational management, it's little surprise that Alan Shearer has been invited to represent the royal family – similarly famed for powerful oratory and uplifting leadership – as deputy lieutenant of Northumberland. I wonder what kind of severance package he's negotiated.

Stoke 0 v United 2 (Berbatov 62, O'Shea 77)

United: Foster, O'Shea, Ferdinand, Vidić, Evra, Valencia, Fletcher, Scholes (Carrick 80), Nani (Giggs 55), Rooney (Owen 80), Berbatov. Unused subs: Kuszczak, Neville, Anderson, Evans.

United 2 (Giggs 59, Carrick 78) **v Wolfsburg 1**

United: Kuszczak, O'Shea, Ferdinand, Vidić, Evra, Valencia (Fletcher 82), Carrick, Anderson, Giggs, Rooney, Owen (Berbatov 20). Unused subs: Foster, Brown, Fábio, Scholes, Nani.

Sunderland home 03/10/09

In Glen David Gold's fictional biography of legendary magician Carter the Great, our hero quickly learns that the crucial skill a conjuror must master is that of misdirection. Nowadays, there is no finer exponent of the art than Sir Alex Ferguson.

Although no one bought his criticism of referee Alan Wiley's fitness as anything other than a poor attempt at masking his team's underperformance, it didn't matter. Thousands of words were still consumed asserting the fact, and thousands more exploring the accusation as though it was legitimate, whilst precious few were directed towards his team selection. So effectively, everyone fell for it yet again anyway, victims, yet again, of the arch dissembler.

That Fergie's comments were churlish and incorrect is beyond doubt, but his point about continental referees is not without some validity; the standard is remarkably low, an observation that becomes more evident with almost every European game. In his day, Jeff Winter was one of the very worst, but nonetheless I was interested to read what he had to say this week – words I never thought anyone would ever write, least of all me. Anyway, hidden within the usual self-promoting drivel was this:

"I think referees will be so incensed about this that Sir Alex may find that United no longer get the benefit of the doubt on certain decisions."

Clearly we need to take anything he says with an enormous pinch of lard – after all, this is a man who thought that an end of season ovation from The Kop was partly in his honour. But if there's something he might know about that we don't, then it's this, and what a *this* it is: according to Winter, the game is currently bent in United's favour, and as a result of Fergie's outburst, we should expect it to become bent the other way. He went on to suggest that Wiley sue for defamation, but perhaps his ex-colleagues should be suing him.

The notion of institutional favouritism has long been a staple of the vanquished, and this seems a suitable occasion to explore it. Thus, consider:

Eric Cantona responded violently to an individual fan who insulted him, and was banned for nine months, but when Didier Drogba violently threw a coin into a crowd aimed at whoever it happened to hit, he was banned for three games; Craig Bellamy, unprovoked, assaulted a supporter during a game and was fined, but when Patrice Evra was incited by a member of Chelsea's groundstaff during a warm-down, his attempted assault resulted in a four game suspension; Roy Keane admitted deliberately injuring an opponent in his autobiography, for which he was banned for five games, but when Michael Owen did the same in his, nothing happened; Christian Negouai missed a drug test and was fined £2000, but when Rio Ferdinand did so a few weeks later, the FA suspended him for eight months.

As Rio himself might say, res ipsa loquitor.

Regarding refereeing decisions, from my perspective – certainly biased, but also pretty extensively researched – for every bum one in United's favour, there's at least another that goes the other way. The difference in perception is because generally, the latter is neither crucial nor repeated on television more times than *Mary Poppins*.

The game against Sunderland encapsulated this in perfect microcosm. During the first half, Andy Reid appeared to handle the ball in his own area, but nothing was given. ESPN's commentators then watched a replay, agreed it was a penalty, and didn't mention it again.

If Old Trafford is as quiet as people say, then it's hard to believe that any visiting officials can be intimidated by 76,000 fans; in fact it's often appeared as though they're more intimidated by the outcry should they give United a marginal decision. You'd expect a team that spends sustained periods in opposition penalty boxes to receive significantly more penalty kicks than other teams, yet they do not. And when United are away, referees have to contend with tighter, usually half-empty grounds, now full of fans apoplectic with unreal rivalry – even though, like any home advantage advantage, its existence is an imaginary construct that preys on the mentally frail.

There's a notion that some officials are scared of upsetting Fergie, but it can also work the other way. On Saturday, the only plausible explanation for no time being appended to the minimum of four added minutes, despite United scoring during it, is that Wiley couldn't be doing with the hassle that'd follow another seemingly impossible turnaround.

But as with the unawarded penalty, that's just not why we didn't win. As fighters are fond of saying, never leave it in the hands of the judges. If you do, you deserve what you get.

And United deserved what they got. Resting players now to keep them fresh for later may have become a necessity, but if you get too cocky in the process, occasionally you'll be shown up. Fergie was silly not to start at least one of Anderson and Carrick, in the groove after excellent midweek efforts, and the omission from the squad of his emergency Giggs, particularly with an international break imminent, was utterly inexplicable. On the plus side, it was nice to see Welbeck given a game, even if it wasn't in his natural position, just a shame that he was let down by teammates whose collective display was as poor as poverty.

If this was unforeseeable, the contribution of Foster certainly was not, his mistakes punished in points for the first time. Whilst not saving the excellent early shot that gave Sunderland their first goal was forgivable, mincing away from the cross that led to their second was not. Physical shirking is never acceptable, and must be punished severely; I hope Micky Phelan tied him naked to a goalpost and got Scholes and Rooney over to do some shooting practice.

For the last few seasons, home games against middling sides have been won fairly comfortably, Ronaldo's remarkable knack for delivering morale-crushing early goals not giving the others much of a chance to underperform. At the start of the season it was suggested that the team might struggle to score in his absence, but in fact they're finding it easier; the problem is keeping them out. Form's obviously a factor, but the configuration of the team is another; with its major source of goals gone, others have taken on greater attacking responsibility and the team is set up to facilitate that; good.

Sunderland, of course, played very well, though will be disappointed that their best wasn't enough to beat United's worst. I promised myself I wouldn't mention Kieran Richardson and his pigtail, but just when you thought the man with the most hittable face in football couldn't look any more stupid, he goes and gets himself sent off in the way that he did. He really is thicker than a five dollar shake full of scousers.

Moving away from United, FIFA vice-president Jack Warner made the headlines this week after he panned England's World Cup bid, and what a truly devastating panning it was:

"I came here and was shocked that I got a bag for Australia at the entrance...why isn't there a bag for England?"

Ah, presents for freeloaders, the cornerstone of any successful tournament. And there's more:

"My colleagues are saying very quietly that the guys who are coming to them are lightweight. This is the type of thing that loses you a bid...If I had the Premier League, Beckham and the Queen there would have been many things I could have done for the people who are voting".

Yes, apparently it's also important that said freeloaders meet their favourite celebrities, rather than waste their valuable speaking to those running the bid.

Most telling, though, is his advice to be "more aggressive in the market place". At last, something we can take in good faith. You see, market place aggression – unlike organising World Cups – is something in which Mr Warner has no little expertise. After the last such competition, for example, Ernst & Young – FIFA's auditors – estimated that his family made a profit of almost $1 million selling tickets on the black market. All the misdirection in the world shouldn't distract us from that.

United 2 (Berbatov 51, Ferdinand o.g. 90+4) **v Sunderland 2**

United: Foster, O'Shea, Vidić, Evans, Evra, Nani, Fletcher (Carrick 71), Scholes (Anderson 46), Welbeck (Valencia 71), Rooney, Berbatov. Unused subs: Kuszczak, Fábio, Brown, Ferdinand.

International week 09/10/09

"I'm a firm believer in the philosophy of a ruling class", surmised legendary thinker Randal Graves, "especially since I rule". Whether he was advocating the purest anarchy or most virulent oligarchy is open to interpretation, and the footballing world appears similarly divided on the matter.

Pursuing the former is Football Club United of Manchester. Conceived in early 2005 as an option in the event of a takeover, the idea was supported by many intending to boycott but unwilling to be deprived of their United fix. A few months later, the club was born, with the aim – despite perceptions to the contrary – of running alongside, rather than in opposition to its bigger brother.

But the Glazer takeover was only a tipping point, serving to highlight the other liberties – early kick-offs, heavy-handed stewarding and ridiculous pricing – that had been largely ignored through the previous decade because their encroachment was incremental and the football so good. The reality, though, was that the action had become the only enjoyable element of the 90 minutes, so FC set about revitalising the matchgoing experience as an outlet for well-intentioned unruliness.

Ok, the name's a bit of a mouthful, but what can you do? The words "Manchester" and "United" needed to be there, as did "Football" and "Club", their removal from the crest of Big United symbolic of its manipulation from fellowship into brand. But don't hate on the name, feel the acronym.

And anyway, though it could scan better, there were no complaints, because everyone who cared about it voted for it; the ruling class is everyone, and they all rule. The club is owned by its members, and not just in theory; ticket pricing is determined by a vote, and those on the board are elected, not appointed. Run according to the Industrial & Provident Society Model as a not-for-profit organisation, the club is obligated to no one but itself and exists solely for its own ends.

Those ends, though, are by no means selfish. From its inception, FC has attempted to fill the space in the community that was once occupied by United. Going to the game is cheap enough to exclude no one, the focus is on developing talent rather than buying it in, and the work done with local youth is at least the relative equal of anything done at Old Trafford.

Sadly, examples of supporter activism are rare in this country, fighting the power coming a distant third behind apathy and rivalry. The German model, on the other hand – where fans of different clubs co-ordinate protests about specific issues that matter to many – has led to reduced ticket pricing, stadia with safe standing areas, and match highlights shown on free-to-air television a couple of hours after full-time.

Achieving this in England is difficult only because there is no coherence between the fans of different clubs. If parochialism could be briefly put aside for the greater good, then its continued enjoyment in a suitable environment would be far more likely than it is now.

In the meantime, we may as well enjoy the occasional minor victory. This weekend's game against Bolton is United's first home Saturday three o'clock in almost a year, leaving me with a choice of either pub or internet – how very apt. After years of disenfranchising matchgoers with the tyranny of television, the FA are now being repaid in kind, and well do they deserve it.

But it's not just the FA who are guilty of negatively applying Graves' aphorism. This was exemplified most recently by FIFA's decision to seed the draw for the playoff games that will determine the final World Cup qualifiers from the European zone. As a neutral, I'd prefer the best players to be involved, but only if they deserve to be. Currently, the likes of Ronaldo and Ribery deserve a randomly drawn playoff against another country that could only finish second in its group, because that's all they were able to deliver for theirs.

Had the seeding been the intention from the start, it would still have been wrong, but at least it would've been the system. Instituting it once it became clear some of the bigger names were struggling, is, as Daffy Duck would love to say, fucking despicable. But sadly, and yet again, money is prioritised over the integrity of competition.

Talking of folding green ones, Ryan Giggs was quoted this week as having said the following:

"The average player is getting a lot of money – if that is right, I don't know".

Well, Ryan, allow me to enlighten you: it isn't. No one minds too much that the best players are paid huge sums – they are in most sports, as are the best in the world at most objects of human endeavour. But the amount of money thrown at mediocrities and young players is close to immoral. Why should supporters pay for El-Hadji Diouf to park his gold Cadillac in a loading bay and not care if he gets a ticket? What teenager wouldn't be affected by the sudden ability to afford and attract as much of anything as he and his friends could ever want?

This isn't 'Nam, so let's have a few rules. If basic pay were lower and bonuses higher, obscene money would at least be some kind of reward. Young players would then have to earn their wealth, rather than be presented with it while on the fringes of a team that's keeping them just in case they turn out to be good.

On which point it was nice to see that after all these years, Fergie has finally learnt how to tap someone up without infringing the rules. Sending a letter to Liège's Steven Defour wishing him a speedy recovery is nothing new, and to read it you'd think he was suffering from ebola, rickets and gangrene all mixed into one – but doing it via his club is a lovely touch. In obliging them to pass it on, they've alerted the player to United's interest, but can't have any complaints because they told him of it themselves.

Realistically, though, this is about as good as it'll get. There's no way of stopping people talking to each other, so there's no way of stopping tapping. The best we can hope for is that it's done in public – then at least everyone knows what's what, which I suppose in the shady world of football counts as some sort of result.

Bolton home 17/10/09

CSKA Moscow away 21/10/09

A United end dominated by loud Russian voices isn't something I thought I'd ever hear, but with only 250 making the trip to Moscow, the remainder of the allocation went to more local types, imploring Fergie to "give me away".

It was a bit like hearing Alexandra Burke singing *Hallelujah*; odd sounding, but hard to dislike in a sharing the wealth kind of benevolence. In any event, their enthusiasm enlivened a fairly dull evening, so nice one Cyrillics.

As a Londoner, I was almost envious of their lack of shame in instantly outing themselves as non-Mancunians, remembering the self-conscious years of my youth spent fearful of revealing my generic southern accent. As it happens, this was largely a reflection of my own insecurity; United fans have always been proud of the club's universal appeal, despite some of its unfortunate by-products.

Even though glory hunters of my generation follow Liverpool, I'm regularly called upon to justify my affiliation, which I assume isn't a roundabout way of complimenting me on how young I look. Whenever I'm asked which team I support, my answer almost always precipitates a further question challenging my right so to do. This is inevitably followed by a grudging acceptance when I reveal that my dad's from Cheetham Hill, and his dad had a season ticket in the 30s, 40s and 50s – as though the legitimacy of my identity is somehow within their gift.

Whilst I have what is generally deemed to be fair reason, I still rail on behalf of those who don't. How could any young boy fail to be seduced by what United represent if he had no other footballing imperative forced upon him? As Rakim said and Ian Brown later repeated, "it ain't where you're from, it's where you're at".

This is precisely the reason why no one cares when opposition fans – often those of Woolwich Arsenal – come to Old Trafford and sing things like "City come from Manchester". Regardless of what borough the ground happens to be in, serial winners famed for fortitude and panache encapsulate Manc attitude far better than perennial losers forever bragging about what they're about to do.

Anyway, to the football. The game against CSKA was similar to the one at Beşiktaş, United largely in control without really threatening, the goal expected at some point or other arriving late on. It was, though, a little disappointing not to have the fixture in December when it's properly cold – partly for my own gratification, partly to see the players suffer.

As it happens, they've shown real enthusiasm in recent weeks, which as fans, we feel we should take for granted. And so we should, but it's also worth remembering that as soon as hobby becomes work, a person's relationship to it changes, even if it's still a hobby. There was a time when every day I would salivate at the mere prospect of writing, but the moment it became my job, and even though I don't love it any less, it is now indisputably a chore.

And I can see why shlepping to Moscow is a chore, the game arousing not even the slightest anticipation, the result irrelevant to the eventual outcome of the group. Unable to find and take revenge on the police horse that bit me the last time I was at the Luzhniki, the major plus point was the performance of Fábio. Both he and his twin – who unfortunately isn't called Grooverider – play with an absolute absence of fear, and though it would be better if they were from Gorton or Collyhurst, Rio's a decent alternative.

Of course the midweek fixture was only a warm-up to Sunday's serious business against Liverpool. A few years ago in the build-up to the game, 5 live interviewed a fanzine bod from either side, which provided a neat illustration of why Mancs and Scousers don't get on. Asked as to the root of the rivalry, the United delegate delivered an erudite exposition of historical, geographical, sociological and economic factors, to which Liverpool's responded with "nah, it's all about the football, la".

This dichotomy is also reflected in the playing philosophies of the clubs. For United, it's essential to win with style, whereas for Liverpool it's essential only to win. Our European Cup triumph over Chelsea, for example, is forever tainted by the penalty shoot-out that earned it, whereas their victories in Rome and Istanbul are central pillars of their mythology.

From a United perspective, the question this Sunday is dare we win? No Red in his right mind wants to see the end of Benítez's able stewardship, but what an opportunity awaits – the joy of not only kicking them while they're down, like Shogun Rua in his pomp, but of grinding them into gristle, cackling maniacally at the sadistic violence of it all.

Poor old Benítez. Just when he thought his week had reached its nadir, it got worse, the ignominy of being publicly and justifiably criticised by Jermaine Pennant bestowed on very few. A player whose touch was so awry I thought he'd forgotten to remove his tag, Pennant is but one of the many unpleasant uselessnesses Benítez has sold at a loss, all the while moaning about the paucity of his transfer kitty.

Like those of Arsenal and Chelsea, the quality of Liverpool's squad actually reflects very well on Fergie, who has, since the Forlán-Bellion-Djemba-Djemba-Kléberson-Miller embarrassment, been on the money with almost every signing. The current collection may still be a couple of outstanding attackers light, with no discernible first eleven, but what it does have is range.

With each player bringing something different to the team, the horses for courses approach – though frustrating – does generally work, and there are always game-changing options on the bench for when it doesn't, explaining in part the rediscovery of the late goal phenomenon so vital during the 90s.

Meanwhile, the reserves also look very strong. Given the sins Fergie has excused in the past, you can only wonder what Zoran Tošić has done to offend him, his exclusion – even from League Cup games – completely unfathomable. In the last couple of weeks, the now-fit Gabriel Obertan has excelled as well, showing physical strength, the ability to play off both feet and a sharp footballing brain – unsurprising given the size of his head.

Jonny Evans is another young player who looks to have something about him. Although he's yet to convince completely, I was particularly keen on what he had to say earlier this week:

"Because it was my first real season I made a conscious decision to play it really safe and just concentrate on defending above all else. This year I need to try and get on the ball, and really try to express myself a bit more".

The man he may eventually replace would do well to take note. Those who remain underwhelmed by Rio Ferdinand's defensive ability have dwindled in number, but no one can argue that his attacking contribution has been a disappointment. Billed from a very young age as a ball-playing libero in the mould of Beckenbauer and Sammer, he's neither auxiliary playmaker nor reliable goalscorer. Whether the fault lies with him or his manager is unclear, but full marks to Evans for wanting to do better.

To finish, three things that amused me this week: one, a temper tantrum from self-confessed "big man" John Terry, literally jumping up and down with infantile rage after Villa's winning goal; two, Glen Johnson protecting his balls rather than his keeper as Darren Bent lined up his beachball cannon trick shot; and three, reading that Aly Cissokho failed a medical at Milan on account of his teeth. Bearing in mind they signed Ronaldinho, that is quite some achievement.

United 2 (Knight o.g. 5, Valencia 33) **v Bolton 1**

United: van der Sar, Neville, Ferdinand, Evans, Evra (O'Shea 83), Anderson (Scholes 86), Carrick, Valencia, Berbatov, Giggs, Owen (Welbeck 83). Unused subs: Brown, Nani, Macheda, Kuszczak.

CSKA Moscow 0 v United 1 (Valencia 86)

United: van der Sar, Neville, Ferdinand (Brown 57), Vidić, Fábio (Carrick 88), Scholes (Owen 71), O'Shea, Valencia, Anderson, Nani, Berbatov. Unused subs: Kuszczak, Welbeck, Evans, Macheda.

Liverpool away 25/10/09

Barnsley away 27/10/09

"Some things in life are bad, they can really make you mad. Other things just make you swear and curse…like Fergie's team selection". Ok, it's actually "like traffic lights", but they've got nothing on the man nicknamed Tinkerbell long before Ranieri bumbled onto our radar. As frustrated as a mute at a pantomime, I flailed and railed on discovering we would play Liverpool with Carrick and Scholes in midfield; horses for courses is all very well, but only when you pick the right ones.

Painfully lost in the corresponding fixture last season, these days Scholes is effective only when given space or as the furthest forward of a midfield five, whilst Carrick needs pace up front to properly exploit the quickness of his eye and accuracy of his passing. Individually they weren't actually that bad, but the partnership was entirely unsuitable, the running power to get beyond the strikers particularly important against a side with two spoilers stationed directly in front of the back four.

Thus the total exclusion of Anderson's energy and ball-carrying ability was inexplicable. With the wide players isolated on the touchline, the front two received nowhere near enough support, the team unable to work the sharp passing that undoes diligent defending and makes it far harder to foil attacks solely by weight of numbers.

There are those who think that whatever their merits as individuals, the Rooney-Berbatov pairing will never work, but the way it matches instinct with intellect is reminiscent of the Hughes-Cantona partnership of the 90s. The key is surrounding it with qualities that amplify its strengths rather than exacerbate its weaknesses.

This does not include selecting O'Shea at right-back. With Aurelio on the left of Liverpool's midfield, there was no danger of Gary Neville's lack of pace being exposed, and one of the most striking things about the previous two games was the difference he made as an auxiliary attacker.

Similarly, though Rafael was probably not far enough into his comeback to be considered, his brother may nominally be a left-back, but he's right-footed, and would have been a far braver pick than the limited, lipided O'Shea. Both twins are ready to play regularly, and it's about time they were given the chance. The way many teams defend against United, the full-backs see a lot of the ball, and these two know what to do when they get it.

Although Liverpool were the better team on Sunday and deserved their victory, the referee seems to have escaped censure for a very poor performance (and what sort of referee's name is Andre Mariner anyway?). There doesn't seem much point in discussing the non-dismissal of Carragher nor the ten fouls Lucas committed without being booked, but the penalty United were denied just before half-time is worth another look.

Carrick, for the only time in the game, burst into the Liverpool box. Sliding in with a desperate lunge, Carragher's leg went over the ball, tickling it with his heel, the rest of him ploughing straight through the United player and bringing him down.

How is this not a penalty? Had Carragher won possession then fine, but he didn't; Carrick remained in prime position to shoot. For the same reason, controversial penalties awarded last season – one against Heurelho Gomes and one against Darren Fletcher – were both correct, even though the players in question made far more significant contact with the ball than did Carragher. As Fergie admitted, this wasn't why we lost (though doubtless he doesn't think it his fault either), but the laws do not state that all violence is permitted provided it is preceded by the faintest touch on the ball.

Anyway, time to leave Liverpool to their pyrrhic victories and purple wheelies. That team will not be champions, even if we have to feel relieved each time Chelsea win for a while longer yet.

The pace and imagination of the younger players made the midweek game at Barnsley a lot more enjoyable. With nods to Welbeck, Tošić, Fábio and Rafael, Obertan was the stand-out performer; simply watching him move with the ball is enough to make it clear that he's a natural.

Initially I was worried upon discovering that my phone's spellcheck corrected his name to Overran; I'm used, you see, to Painles and Highs, Scholes and Giggs respectively. But I needn't have worried; his range of skills very obviously mark him out as miles better than most of United's other wide options, and he needs to play in the first team forthwith.

Although I remained in my seat, transfixed by the glitz, glam and razzmatazz of the cheerleading display, I suppose I'd better mention the half-time concourse shenanigans. If nothing else, we must be glad of the commotion for eliciting this quotation from a member of Barnsley's canteen staff:

"I feared for my life when the door to the food and beverage distribution point was kicked off its hinges. Around 20–30 louts headed for the pie section and helped themselves...it was a terrifying experience, I have had to take the rest of the week off work and I don't feel like working at Oakwell again until after Christmas."

Now nicking pies is obviously illegal, but in the pantheon of football violence, it's not exactly up there, is it? A few stolen baltis hardly translate into a reason to apprehend imminent death, and I'm sure there are plenty of us who wouldn't mind skiving work until January.

I don't say this to be flippant, but to draw attention to the reality of the situation. Football fans are boisterous, that boisterousness a large part of what makes an atmosphere, one of the reasons so many people go to watch. I've never been in a fight in my life, least of all at the game, but I wouldn't be dishonest enough to deny that the confrontational mood is something I enjoy. Inevitably, it occasionally gets out of hand, but the furore over a few people helping themselves after they were refused service has been a lot much.

What is of genuine note is that as the game meandered to a close, out of nowhere trooped a troupe of fancy dress riot police – no doubt on overtime – in one of the most unnecessary wastes of taxes imaginable. And to rub it in, a line of aggressive Alsatians soon followed them, backed up by a load of horses that turned raised eyebrows into outright incredulity, even more so when none of them did anything to stop the home fans who subsequently invaded the pitch.

For some reason, a League Cup tie with Barnsley was deemed to require a more significant police presence than a game at Anfield, woefully undermanned for the second consecutive season. Enjoyable for some, but painful for a fair few minding-their-own-business others ambushed by groups of crew-cutted Scousers, presumably reacting against the perms that made the lovable scamps such international trendsetters. But why devote a column inch or airtime second to reporting it when people are robbing pies? Won't somebody please think of the steak and kidneys!

Saturday sees the arrival at Old Trafford of Sam Allardyce, everyone's favourite paragon of maltreatment. He was in the news earlier in the week after Roberto Martinez – in a laughable attempt to play with the big boys – reportedly gobbed off to a Spanish paper, accusing Fergie of moulding his managerial counterparts into a cabal of yes-men, tantalising Allardyce in particular with the prospect of the United job when he retires. What an entirely ridiculous notion; surely not even he can be that oblivious?

The Big One himself has indulged in a good whinge about the swine flu epidemic that's affecting his Blackburn squad, keeping away from his players before the Peterborough game after experiencing some symptoms himself; oh how they wept! It was therefore surprising to see him watching from the stand – clearly it matters only that footballers are protected from his lurgy.

This attitude would find favour with the horrible Marlon King, jailed yesterday and whom a law reporter pal of mine witnessed being aggressive to the automated voice in the courtroom lift. Promptly sacked by Wigan, the cavity search was barely underway before his agent was on the radio, crowing nastily about how easily he would find him another club on his release. Wigan chairman Dave Whelan was soon interviewed too, praising himself for acting on behalf of the younger fans to whom such a bad example had been set. Yes Dave, I'm sure as King begins an 18-month stretch for sexual assault, kids the length and breadth of the land are aspiring to be him, and you – yes you – have saved them. Bravo!

Finally, the Glazer gimps were in the country this week, watching Tampa take a pasting from New England. Unfortunately schadenfreude was tempered by fear at the potential knock-on effect, especially with sources in Tampa suggesting that the Glazers are looking to sell the franchise. Having denied reports that they lost $400 million in the Madoff scandal – although the legal action threatened against those who've said otherwise has yet to materialise – their exposure to the banks that financed their purchase of United is rumoured to be the most significant motivation behind any such move. The Bucs, who left $30 million of their allotted salary budget unspent, remain winless this season.

I think that brings us back to the mute…

Liverpool 2 v United 0

United: van der Sar, O'Shea, Ferdinand, Vidić, Evra, Valencia, Carrick, Scholes (Nani 74), Giggs, Rooney, Berbatov (Owen 74). Unused subs: Foster, Neville, Evans, Fábio, Anderson. Sent off: Berbatov.

Barnsley 0 v United 2 (Welbeck 6, Owen 59)

United: Foster, Neville, Brown, Evans, Fábio, Obertan, Rafael, Anderson, Welbeck (Tošić 53), Owen (de Laet 66), Macheda. Unused subs: Amos, O'Shea, C Evans, King, James. Sent off: Neville.

Blackburn home 31/10/09

CSKA Moscow home 03/11/09

When I was a lad, it was generally held that the most inappropriate behaviour imaginable was sex with the rabbi's wife over the synagogue reading desk – at least until someone threw piss over the bloke leading the service. But then this week, Harry Redknapp decided it was his place to dispense instruction as to what constitutes acceptable behaviour.

Anyway, I'll get to that presently, but let's deal with the football first. Luckily I got stuck in traffic on my way home to watch the Blackburn game, so that by the time I got there I had a fair bit of juice saved up on Sky+, the double speed making the carelessly slow start less painful than for those watching in real time. Though the win was routine in the end, the incredibly poor quality of the set-pieces was even more annoying than usual – perhaps United should replace Micky Phelan with Quentin Tarantino.

Also this week we've seen another couple of promising shows from Obertan, encouragingly looking to play around defenders, and not just from the touchline. The upside of this upside is that it should facilitate the binning of Nani. He may never have had a proper run in the team, but neither has he earned one, and it's inconceivable that he could attain the level of performance required to mitigate his cheating, truculence and perpetually indignant expression. As frustrating as a pair of rubber pants, I doubt there'd be a single person mithered if he left and plenty who'd happily give him a boot in the right direction.

Sunday's game at Chelsea is a rare occasion on which it's more important not to lose than it is to win, a fact I hope Fergie hasn't noticed. The return of Fletchinho will give the midfield some ballast and urgency, and you can only trust that the temptation to supplement it with all of Anderson, Carrick, Giggs and Valencia is ignored. After a year waiting for Berbatov to supply brilliant goals at crucial moments, there've been two in the last few weeks, and having also made John Terry look silly on more than a couple of occasions, his selection is imperative.

And how very apt it is that in this week of remembrance, we mention Brave John Terry, champion of the armed forces:

"They love their football. They like to look up to us, but I would like to be in their shoes and do what they do...I would love to, of course. Put your life on the line for the country – I would love to".

Now I'm not saying this isn't true, but the available evidence certainly suggests that perhaps it might not be. Unless, of course, he tried to join up and the army decided it wasn't really looking for the sort of recruits who disintegrate under pressure and cry when they miss a penalty.

Terry's tears, of course, were the major redeeming beauty of a European Cup won Scouse-style; it's rare, in any context, that you get to witness an event that causes someone a lifetime's worth of torment, and even rarer when that event doesn't hurt you as much as it hurts them. After United's win over City earlier in the season, Sky screened a vomit-inducing "home with JT" spot, during which Terry admitted that he thinks about his missed penalty "30 or 40 times a day". I guarantee he will have no trouble surpassing this target on Sunday.

Talking of City, I see that Ricky Hatton paraded in a Stoke shirt last weekend, finally exposing a myth that's lasted longer than the Gallaghers'. Not that you can blame them; where else would hype-seeking Mancunians turn, but to the gullible tenants of Eastlands?

City and their ill-gotten gains have made Liverpool's miserable week marginally less amusing than it might otherwise have been; we'll probably be relying on them to stop the Bitters sneaking the Champions League qualification that'll help bribe some decent players. But how not to laugh at the effrontery of Jamie Carragher in protesting a justly awarded red card, nor the muttering, twitching, sweating mess that is Benítez, illustrating exactly why it is that cooks demand waiters stay out of kitchens.

Talking of managers looking silly brings us back to good old 'Arry, proving this week that history doesn't just repeat itself as farce the second time around, but the third, fourth and fifth as well, all the way to infinity and beyond. Arsenal's victory may have been bad for United, but there was still enjoyment to be had in how quickly Redknapp's pre-match boasts were shown up for the nonsense we all knew they were anyway, his side taking yet another well-deserved thumping. And as ever, excuses were to the fore; yes Harry, but for the tiny details of bad defending, bad goalkeeping and bad concentration…you'd still have lost.

Anyway, I also promised a bit more on Redknapp's guide to clean living, so here it is. In *Broken Dreams*, Tom Bower's meticulously researched look at questionable business practice in English football, only one man is considered worthy enough to merit a chapter devoted solely to his achievements; can you guess who it is?

And yet Redknapp appears to view himself as some kind of moral crusader, regularly – and this week once again – mouthing off about the unacceptable behaviour of the scum who populate football grounds. So let's break it down. Redknapp defected from Portsmouth to Southampton after promising he wouldn't, then returned to Portsmouth, before dumping them the second a better job became available. Some people took exception to this behaviour.

It's inconceivable that when he made those decisions, he didn't consider the likely reaction, a con he accepted in exchange for the not inconsiderable pro of becoming an even more incredibly rich man than before. And in the same way he did as he pleased regardless of what supporters thought, those supporters will reciprocate in the only forum available to them.

When Luís Figo left Barcelona for Madrid – an act of treachery that dwarfs Redknapp's – the first time he visited his old ground, a pig's head was thrown at him. But rather than bleat about the unfairness of it all, he ignored it. He knew what he was getting himself into, and that what he did constituted tacit acceptance of the inevitable backlash.

And in any case, on whose behalf is Redknapp acting? Generally, he legitimises his whining by presupposing the effect of the vitriol directed at him on other people's children, even though he seems to be the only person who has a problem with it. But taking him at face value for a moment, the ability to swear freely and shout abuse is something that attracts young people to the match. Whether it's becoming for a man to do so in front of his kids is a fair question to ask, but it's certainly not for Redknapp to prescribe the answer.

Were I a player or a manager, the crowd could swear at me, insult my mother and laugh at my appearance as much as they like, and I'd never react, because I wouldn't be in the least bit bothered (sorry Mum). They don't know me, I don't know them, who cares what we think of one another?

And what happens should the FA actually take action? Would there be a list of what it's ok to sing? And what about if songs deemed unacceptable were tempered with negatives or irony – "the referee is not a wanker", for example. Would that become punishable too?

In life, lots of things get said that are unpleasant, at football matches and everywhere else. But restricting free speech requires a far better reason than "I don't like it" or "it's not very nice".

The essential fact that so many players, managers and lawmakers seem unable to grasp is that football isn't just about what happens on the pitch; it's about the relationship between supporters of the same clubs and supporters of different clubs, to which results are just a sideshow; the game belongs to the fans, whatever Companies House records might say. The chanting of the crowd is central to what makes football special, and obnoxious songs – particularly those that are magnificently merited – are part of its charm. If I were a player or manager, it would be all I could do to stop myself spending all day every day convulsing with laughter at my insanely good fortune. Perhaps the likes of Redknapp should think about that the next time someone like me calls them a fucking whinging, grasping, untrustworthy, ballsac-faced cunt.

United 2 (Berbatov 55, Rooney 87) **v Blackburn 0**

United: van der Sar, O'Shea, Brown, Evans, Evra, Anderson, Carrick, Nani Obertan 63), Valencia, Berbatov (Owen 79), Rooney. Unused subs: Kuszczak, Fábio, de Laet, Fletcher, Scholes.

United 3 (Owen 29, Scholes 84, Shennikov o.g. 90+3)
v CSKA Moscow 3

United: van der Sar, Neville, Brown, Evans, Fábio (Evra 59), Valencia, Scholes, Gibson, Nani (Rooney 58), Owen, Macheda (Obertan 82). Unused subs: Kuszczak, O'Shea, Anderson, Gibson.

Chelsea away 08/11/09

Fergie clearly doesn't like Radiohead, because if he did, he'd know to leave the karma police to their own devices. Instead, he criticised Alan Wiley's fitness, provoking the inevitable retaliation. "This is what you get when you mess with us" indeed.

Were I to believe in karma, this would be in some way placating, but I don't, so it isn't. That leaves me with coincidence and luck, not enough to fully explain why in games against Liverpool and Chelsea, United have been on the wrong end of almost every decision remotely givable against them. That isn't to say I'm suggesting any kind of collusion – Martin Atkinson is hardly Edmond Dantès – but neither is it controversial to state that if you continually aggravate people, they'll become subconsciously prejudiced against you. If Fergie were on trial, you'd not be finding Brian Hill, David Elleray and Phil Dowd in the jury.

The probable goal and definite penalty Sunday's linesman denied United was enough to make you wonder what the point of them is, though in any case, the limitations of human vision mean that giving offside will almost always be a matter of judgement rather than of fact. This doesn't especially bother me, but on behalf of those eager to eliminate human error, you'd think that the technology exists for each player's boot to be fitted with a sensor, linked to a receiver on the touchline able to tell us definitively what's on and what's off.

The other major point of contention was Chelsea's winner, in the course of which they received the benefit of three consecutive calls.

Perhaps it was a foul on Cole – always to be applauded – but once the resultant free kick came in, two subsequent infringements were missed. I appreciate it's crowded in there and that things happen quickly, but you'd expect at least one of the officials to notice at least one of them, and act upon it.

That said, they can't have been expected to clear the cross, which in a sense is the crucial point. Despite being the smoother, more imaginative side, United didn't play well enough to guarantee victory regardless of refereeing incompetence, though losing with that caveat was far less annoying than losing as a result of not turning up, as happened against Liverpool.

Prior to the game, the majority of the focus had been on Chelsea's purported superiority, the speculation about what might happen should United be badly beaten. That was never likely, a ropey display at Anfield evidence of nothing other than a ropey display at Anfield. The best performance I've seen so far this season, and by a long way, was United's at Spurs, and there's been enough other examples of quality to suggest that the team's the right selection away from being extremely handy.

A fair amount of chatter surrounded its depleted back four, also misdirected. When Wes Brown is fit and paying attention, he's an exceptional defender able to cope with the very best attackers, and his performance in the second leg of the Barca semi in 2008 is easily the best individual effort from a United defender in the last few seasons.

Next to him, Jonny Evans has already done well enough enough times to look like he might be up to the task regularly, a proper footballer playing with the assurance of someone who knows he can do it. Excellent but flawed last season, generally much better this, he competes with an intelligence that you'd expect from someone with 4A* and 5As, and yes, despite falling standards, typing that gave me a lot of pleasure.

Playing a position that takes longer to master than Othello, his consistency is no small achievement. Rio Ferdinand, for example, had been identified as a talent from a very young age, but was 24 before he was anywhere near established. It's also nice to see two reserves, both United schooled, able to step in and excel. Had Ancelotti any sense, he'd have piled Drogba and Anelka on top of O'Shea and told the others to come from deep, but then had he any sense he'd also not have devised a midfield configuration that emaciates the attributes of all who play in it – irrelevant against rubbish but significant against another decent outfit.

Similarly, United's balance is also not quite right. With Giggs enduring an acrylic afternoon and the other midfielders infrequent scorers, it was hard to see where a goal would come from if Rooney didn't deal with it. Some time spent honing the system might change that, even if in the long term this would be at the expense of Berbatov, injured at the weekend.

It'll never happen, but one way around it would be to retain the three-man midfield and use Rooney as its primary attacker, although this might lead to him spending most of the season suspended. The only other way of squeezing in two strikers would be to omit Carrick and go 4–2–3–1.

Otherwise, it'll be important to bring in Obertan for Valencia, who's improving, but doesn't have the variety or versatility necessary to play as one of three floating forwards. With the opposition fielding no discernable left-winger, it would also have been worth being bold and including a more attacking right-back, something I seem to mention almost every week.

In the news after the game was a group of attention-seeking City fans – formed following Adebayor's deserved suspension – with the aim of pointlessly haranguing the FA to punish all others who in their opinion have transgressed; a more ridiculous waste of time you could not wish to see, as Barry Davies might say. It ought to be impossible to believe that people of this ilk exist, but it isn't and they do. I'd always assumed that Del Amitri's "Angry from Manchester" was a City fan, and this proves it.

While I've been sitting writing, two more stories have broken, so a bit about those. Fergie's denigration of Alan Wiley has landed him a two-game touchline ban with a further two suspended, along with a hefty fine, which seems fair enough. But it remains unclear as to what exactly the punishment is for. If it's for making a serious accusation that turned out to be false, then ok, but if it's simply for making a serious accusation, then not ok. People are entitled to speak their mind openly, all the more so when they operate in the public arena, and if they're right, then it's the subject of the complaint who should face sanctions.

Equally troubling is what was said by the silk conducting matters:

"Each member of the commission recognised Sir Alex Ferguson's achievements and stature within the game. Having said that, it was made clear to Sir Alex that with such stature comes increased responsibilities".

Yes, you read that right: according to Peter Griffiths, QC, not only is there no equality before the law, but it applies most strictly to those who have achieved most. Utterly, utterly astonishing – unless, of course, there's something we don't know, and Fergie is actually Peter Parker in disguise.

Meanwhile, the delightful Phil Gartside's altruistic quest to make the Premier League more money has just failed, a majority of clubs vetoing a plan to invite Rangers and Celtic to join. Of course the fringe benefit of ring-fencing investments by doing away with relegation was but a lucky chance. I note, though, that the plan didn't mention redistributing the increased wealth to supporters forced to hike to Scotland twice a season.

In any case, and Berwick Rangers aside, allowing teams to cross borders would set far too dangerous a precedent. From a purely competitive perspective, the Old Firm would probably raise the standard, but then so would Real Madrid and Barcelona. And bearing in mind what's happened when Rangers and Celtic have come to Manchester, the prospect of either one or other infesting England on a weekly basis doesn't sound like a very good way of increasing the peace.

Talking of the Old Firm, a new candidate has emerged for this year's Barry Ferguson Lack of Self-Knowledge Award, the eponymous inaugural recipient honoured for this gem:

"People always say it's a shame someone as talented as Ryan Giggs or George Best before him never played in a World Cup or European Championship and I don't want my name to be added to that list".

Anyway, his mantlepiece now passes to Kevin Davies, following this remarkable proclamation:

"Recently it's been obvious that players have been told to make a meal of any contact and get me taken out of the game."

Actually Kevin, 49 goals in 351 Premier League appearances says that a team featuring you in one of its striking positions is a veritable boon for any opposing team. You are truly a worthy heir.

Chelsea 1 v United 0

United: *van der Sar, O'Shea, Brown, Evans, Evra, Valencia, Carrick, Anderson (Owen 85), Giggs (Obertan 85), Rooney.*
Unused subs: Kuszczak, Vidić, Fábio, Gibson, Scholes.

International week 13/11/09

Referees' Union head Alan Leighton must be related to ex-United goalie Jim; there's simply no other explanation as to why he's continued to prolong the tedium of the Fergie/Wiley saga. Unless, of course, he's parasiting on someone else's fame and is hot, breathless and horny from seeing his name in print.

No sooner was the matter officially closed than Leighton opened it again, publicly speculating as to whether Wiley would sue – a question he'd have been better off discussing with the man himself. He may also have been wise to consult a lawyer, but instead chose to make sure he got in the papers again, at the price of showcasing his ignorance. For a statement to be defamatory – as set out by Lord Atkin in *Sim v Stretch*, in case anyone's interested – it must lower the claimant in the estimation of right-thinking members of society.

So let's look at the evidence: Fergie apologised, pleaded guilty, was punished by an independent body, and unanimously condemned. Very clearly, he was the only person lowered in the estimation of anyone, and for his trouble was hit with a hefty fine and touchline ban – a pretty stern punishment for a remark made in the heat of the moment. But still this wasn't enough for Leighton, wading in yet again lest he be dispatched back to anonymity; expect to see him in the Australian jungle some time in the future, eating wallaby cervix whilst singing *Take A Look At Me Now*.

This would be a whole lot more entertaining than England's "prestige friendly" with Brazil, more boring than a pneumatic drill. It was, though, nice to see Rooney captaining the side. The current United squad has been criticised in the past for a lack of on-pitch leadership, but increasingly that's not the case. Rooney, Evra, Fletcher and Evans are all showing signs not only of the cajoling that's associated with authority, but the consistent excellence that's a lot more important.

In these days of weekly waxing, pre-match preening and half-time hair spiking, the sight of Rooney's chest rug overflowing from his shirt was equally gratifying. Talking of matters sartorial, with humidity in Doha at ridiculous levels, what on earth possessed Fabio Capello to choose a blue shirt? Wear white with a t-shirt underneath and your shvitz might just go unnoticed, wear blue and you look like you're pissing through your pits.

No doubt Rooney will be working up a similar sweat this weekend, with United playing Everton. While the animosity their fans feel towards him is understandable, they'd do well to note his recent declaration that he's still a Toffee and his kids will be too. It's never pleasant to remember that Rooney's a scouse, especially as he appears to get United more than most of his teammates, but there's still something very decent about the implacability of his ultimate loyalty.

Despite starting the season badly, Everton will give United a hard game as they always do, and the defeat at Chelsea has left no margin for error. On that basis, it's handy that we play Beşiktaş in the week, as this'll probably prevent Fergie from selecting Scholes in a game that'll require a different kind of midfield presence. It'd be good for Obertan to be given a start, but likely that too will have to wait until Wednesday.

At the outset, the biggest story of the international break looked like being the Egypt Algeria playoff. An absolute lesson in fanaticism, it was also refreshing to see the game continue with a player down, possibly injured but probably not. During United's game at Stamford Bridge, it was particularly frustrating when Ryan Giggs booted the ball into touch to enable a Chelsea player to receive attention, even though the home team had appealed for the action to stop only after losing possession.

In the event, the France Ireland game elicited the biggest fuss of the week, the overreaction more extreme than Geary, Cherone, Badger and Bettencourt put together. Yes, Henry cheated, but what's new about that? All players do, and a handball is no more dishonest than a foul, especially one with so little disguise.

His celebration, on the other hand, was a different matter. Rather than accept a fortuitous goal with dignity, the world's least sheepish man launched into a performance of je suis le grand homme finger-wagging, compounding it at the final whistle by ostentatiously commiserating with Richard Dunne like some kind of corinthian.

But this should be in no way surprising; Henry happily featured in a commercial alongside Roger Federer and Tiger Woods, company in which he is entirely out of place – presumably Phil "The Power" Taylor was busy that day. He then failed to see any embarrassment in appearing in a sequel that featured Woods and Federer in cartoon form only, Henry poncing and prancing as himself in characteristic fashion.

However just as shameful has been the hand-wringing moralising of the poor put-upon Irish. Fine, they lost by virtue of a bad decision, but the World Cup qualifying campaign has been going on for two years. During that period, they didn't do enough to get there, were given another chance, and again, didn't do enough. The selfishness of calling for a replay, despite the implications – not just for football but for all sport – is staggering, and the FAI should be ashamed of themselves.

What was more heartwarming was Russia losing out to Slovenia, the sole smack in the mouth to FIFA's attempts at rigging the playoffs to the advantage of their favoured nations. This brought with it the additional benefit of expunging the Hiddink myth; one man's inspirational sorcerer is another's lucky mercenary. Anyway, Guus, I'd avoid sushi for a while if I were you.

By a mile the weirdest story of the week was Emmanuel Eboué's admission that "I would like to be Eddie Murphy", a sentence that requires no further garnish. Still, it's fair to say that Arsenal fans and the Nutty Professor would be delighted to see this royal penis trading places, as he'll never feature in their best defence.

And finally, you wait for them for ages and then, rather like Henry handballs, two Barry Ferguson awards come along at once. Hot on the heels of Kevin Davies' entry last week, we were immediately treated to another, courtesy of BBC Radio commentator Alan Green. Interviewed in last Sunday's *Observer*, Green discussed a speech made by Sir Alex Ferguson in honour of Sir Bobby Robson, at BBC's Sports Personality of the Year ceremony:

"Sir Alex came on and his hostility to the BBC is well known and I thought, that's brilliant. He's just pushed that aside because he knows how much it means to Sir Bobby."

Although the pair fell out many years ago, Green nonetheless decided to write Fergie a letter of congratulation, and when no response was forthcoming, took umbrage:

"And I thought, that's just a bit off. I didn't want a reply saying 'Oh, we're going to be best mates now' but I thought he might say thanks for the note."

So let's get this straight: Green was churlish enough to send a letter, not for its own sake but to elicit a particular response that would be pleasing to him. When that response wasn't forthcoming, he instead proclaimed his own magnanimity and used it as a stick with which to beat its intended recipient. And neither does the delusion end there: in Greenland, the most successful manager in the history of the game is expected to care for the approval of a radio commentator who's spent fifteen years revelling in the animosity between them.

If I were Fergie, I'd steer well clear of anyone called Alan.

Everton home 21/11/09

Beşiktaş home 25/11/09

There isn't much that's less United than the Protestant Work Ethic, and in general, neither should there be. But in the case of Darren Fletcher, I'm prepared to make an exception.

Not content with dominating yet another game and scoring the goal of his life in the process, he followed it up by giving an interview quite brilliant in its terseness. Neither affectation nor nervousness, but the natural demeanour of a serious man and a serious footballer, it was all the more puritanical juxtaposed alongside the bouncing effervescence of Patrice Evra, who aptly referred to him only as "Fletcher"; no first name, no nickname, no messing around.

After riding out a difficult start to his career, Fletcher has developed into a player of genuine excellence. Although as a rule, one should never be surprised by anything, there was a time when this would have seemed utterly unfeasible, even if there'd been a United-branded Sword of Thundera on sale in the Megastore.

This monumental improvement raises the question as to what exactly constitutes a player of the highest quality. No one would claim that Fletch has the touch of Fábregas, the goal threat of Gerrard or the power of Essien, but then neither did Roy Keane. And like Keane, Fletch regularly bests all-comers, doing everything very well almost all of the time as much an asset as doing a few things brilliantly. Top Red Andre 3000 was apologising on behalf of United fans everywhere when he said "I'm sorry Darren, woo, you are for reeeaal".

His goal on Saturday was particularly handy, arriving as things were becoming worrisome; despite playing with pace, aggression and control, United had mustered little to make Tim Howard twitch. With Owen performing like he'd won a competition to play for United for the day, seeing Saha on the other side was all the more galling; the best football United – or anyone in England for that matter – has played in the last number of seasons was when he was in the team. Sadly, he took Juvenal too literally, his mind deteriorating with every bodily complaint.

A major plus point of last week was the obvious difference made by a footballing full-back. Comfortable and imaginative enough on the ball to receive possession from a short corner, Rafael's propensity to be caught out of position is a small price to pay for the added attacking dimension he provides. Valencia's continued improvement was also encouraging, his obvious limitations less glaring now he's located some confidence to accompany his biceps. Oddly, most pleasing of all was seeing him blaze a shot from distance over the bar, as previously he'd have meekly squared the ball to someone more senior.

In any case, he's undoubtedly a better option than Park. I must confess that my loneliness is killing me now, but in addition to that, I must also confess that I found it hard to be disappointed by his recent injuries. Although the best football team doesn't have the best player in every position, and although Park is not without use, selecting a winger for his defensive capabilities – especially in big games and especially when there are three in midfield and one up front – is a waste of time and not what United is about.

On that basis, I simply cannot explain why he's been given a four-year deal, unless it's for marketing reasons. With Obertan looking promising, Llajic arriving, Tošić good if he can stop crying, Welbeck able to play wide, and Giggs and Valencia superior, I can't see a scenario in which he'd be required. But of course Fergie will find plenty – such is the problem caused by a large squad full of players in need of time on the pitch.

Thus the midweek game against Beşiktaş was a decent opportunity for those not playing often enough. With so many first team games, reserve leagues no longer comprise those out of form and favour; instead, they're made up of kids and players returning from injury, meaning a far lower level of competition than in previous eras. Consequently, those not getting regular first-team action play hardly at all, Nani's experience last season being a case in point; rarely picked, but around the fringes enough to be denied the chance of improving in the stiffs.

Of those chosen on Wednesday, only Obertan enhanced his reputation, Anderson's lack of arsedness (in all but the physical sense) particularly unhelpful. So too was the incompetence of Foster, who in conceding yet another goal he shouldn't have, allowed the Turks to flood the midfield and defend deep.

Still, United should have done better once behind, forced inside far too easily. As it happens, Macheda was one of those least culpable, but remains so obviously lumbering you'd be unsurprised to see him rolling down the Eagle River with Owen Hargreaves on his back. Strikers that slow have made it before, but require even more exceptional ability than others, and whilst I'm sure he'll go on to have a good career, I'm not sure it'll be at United.

The substitutes sent on to save the day didn't help matters either. Owen managed perhaps a couple of touches in almost half an hour, whilst Carrick either belted the ball out of play or passed it into the arms of the shockingly haggard Rüştü. When the arrival of Inceman, Beşiktaş's splendidly named substitute, is one of the highlights of the game, it's clear that there's not very much to say about it, so I'll stop there.

I will, though, mention Gareth Southgate, chuckling smugly in the studio pre-match about the touchline run-ins he's had with Fergie, forgetting to mention that these were sparked by the vicious assaults of his mardy bunch of useless cloggers. You'd best savour em, Gareth, because you'll not be getting the chance again. Television commentators and analysts are a little like referees; each time you watch a game, you think ah, *this* one's the biggest moron, a judgment that sustains only until the next one.

Talking of televised football, I couldn't help but laugh watching *Match of the Day 2* last Sunday. First we got to hear Jermaine Defoe call Aaron Lennon "Azza" – creativity in the Tottenham dressing room must be limited to eyebrow shaving alone – and then, host Adrian Chiles talked of Sam Allardyce being "pre-op". Now there's an image for you.

Anyway, one more of these while we're at it. Apparently, the "promoters" of Brave John Terry have sent a mass email alerting businesses around the country to their client's desire to harvest money for endorsing a variety of products. Fair enough – who wouldn't want to be associated with a crying, disabled-space parking hero? There's clearly much more to say about this, but due to constraints of space, I'll merely point out that *The Guardian* refer to Terry as "a commercial tool". Sums it up rather nicely, dontcha think?

Just when I thought I'd gone a whole column without laughing at Liverpool, it turns out that I can't help myself. Their game against City last Saturday was a delight, the poverty of both decorated with a result that suited neither. Then, in the lead up to their game against Debrecen, I happened upon this from Jamie Carragher:

"I've spoken to my dad and he said we've had five years of winning big trophies, getting to another Champions League final, going close in the league and that this might just be a difficult season".

Now the wisdom of Carragher senior is beyond doubt – we only have to look at what an articulate, intelligent gentleman his son has become – so it's only fair that it be shared with a wider audience. However it appears he is operating on a conceptual plain that eludes me – I have no idea to which trophies he's referring, nor how a single near miss can span a five-year period.

Talking of renowned gentlemen, Amr Zaki received a small amount of media attention this week for saying the following:

"Joining Portsmouth is no longer an option for me. After Portsmouth signed an Israeli player and also hired an Israeli football director a possible move was ruled out. On top of that, no way could I play at Portsmouth with an Algerian within their ranks".

And this wasn't a comment that was made privately, but one he was happy to publish on his website, for all the world to see. It reminded me of Dick Advocaat's gripe when manager of Zenit St Petersberg:

"I would be happy to sign anyone, but the fans don't like black players. Frankly, the only players who can make Zenit stronger are dark-skinned. But for us it would be impossible. The fans are the most important thing that Zenit have. That's why I have to ask them outright how they'll react if we sign a dark skinned player for Zenit".

So why did Zaki remind me of Advocaat? Because in both cases, despite the almost cartoonish nature of the racism, no one did anything. Kick It Out this, t-shirt that, pennant the other – all posturing, no action. What FIFA needs is Darren Fletcher.

United 3 (Fletcher 35, Carrick 67, Valencia 76) **v Everton 0**

United: van der Sar, Rafael (Scholes 63), Brown, Vidić, Evra, Valencia, Fletcher, Carrick (Gibson 83), Giggs, Rooney, Owen (Obertan 74). Unused subs: Kuszczak, de Laet, Gibson, Welbeck.

United 0 v Beşiktaş 1

United: Foster, Neville, Brown, Vidić, Rafael (Evra, 74), Obertan, Gibson (Carrick 73), Anderson, Park (Owen 69), Macheda, Welbeck. Unused subs: Kuszczak, Nani, Scholes, Fletcher.

Portsmouth away 28/11/09

Spurs home 01/12/09

To paraphrase Verbal Kint, the greatest trick the debt ever pulled was convincing the world it didn't exist. Those who did believe in it were treated as cranks by the vast majority of those in the game and in the media, until the incontrovertible evidence of ticket prices rocketing in inverse proportion to transfer market spending left them looking decidedly Michael Fishy.

For those unfamiliar with great British weather forecasters, Michael Fish was the man who on October 15th 1987 recounted the following:

"Earlier on today, apparently, a woman rang the BBC and said she heard there was a hurricane on the way; well, if you're watching, don't worry, there isn't".

As it turned out, there was – the worst in almost 300 years – and following the sudden abortion of Adem Ljajić's move to United, residents of M16 would do well to brace themselves for a storm.

Quite simply, pulling out of the deal makes sense only against a backdrop of severe financial difficulty. The official line is that there's a coterie of "top young talent" already at the club, in the "attacking midfielder" position, but in fact nothing could be further from the truth; along with pace up front, this is the single most glaring aspect in which the current squad is lacking.

If Ljajić is anywhere near as good as he's meant to be – as good, say, as United thought he was a year ago, when they also thought there was a need for a player of his type – then this excuse is even more of a nonsense. He may not have progressed as expected, but United were undeterred from buying Gabriel Obertan last summer, despite a season far less auspicious than Ljajić's.

There are, of course, two differences; price and economy. Starting with the former, Obertan cost £3 million, Ljajić between three and four times that. The apologists will say that he isn't worth it, and maybe he isn't, but that misses the point. This is Manchester United we're talking about, the most popular club in the world, during one of the most successful periods in its history, in the aftermath of the most profitable summer any team has ever enjoyed, at a time when unimaginable riches are sloshing around the top end of the game. If they have to pay a premium, so what? If the player flops, so what?

In defence of this parsimony, the club preached that in the current market, it was impossible to obtain value for money, hilariously expecting people not to fathom the identity of the most significant beneficiaries of such cursed inflation. For years, Fergie has moaned about the United tax added to the value of any player, before quite rightly paying the necessary – and in the days of Kenyonomics, often necessary plus a load more. Now, suddenly, he expects us to believe in him as ideologue crusader, sacrificing his own needs for the benefit of the world at large.

It's not that I want United to chuck money around for its own sake – there's something very vulgar about using financial might, even that legitimately earned, to liberate talent nurtured by others as soon as convenient. But if absolutely required, the money through the turnstiles demands the need be met, even if it costs more than it should. Instead, we're told about United's proud reputation for developing young players – something the club used to do because it's important, but now is forced into because there's no other choice.

The arrival of this time – always likely given the aggressive tenets of the takeover – has been hastened by the economy. Ljajić had been budgeted for a year ago, and the club applied for a work permit as recently as October, so it seems very much as though United expected to make the payment.

Their sudden refusal so to do illustrates the effrontery of the "top young talent" excuse, as it's impossible anyone has rendered years of scouting worthless by having a good couple of months, however well Cleverley's doing at Watford. I'd suggest the real reason the deal has been pulled is that the recession has hit the Glazers harder than they're letting on; either a planned refinancing is no longer possible, or they require the Ljajić money for something else, perhaps both.

Frighteningly, that something else needn't have anything to do with United – the Glazers are free to urinate cash out of the club and into any interest of theirs that needs it; verily money ain't got no owners, only spenders. And who knows what they might do next time they're short?

Meanwhile, Fergie – who unforgivably welcomed the Glazers in the first place – skives his weekly press conference, safe in the knowledge that he can be boozing and spieling a merry retirement by the time we're in real trouble.

It's possible that Ljajić will turn out to be another Celio Silva, and that United spend the money on a better, similar player. But until they do, the evidence does not look good. Promoting himself – sorry, I mean England's World Cup bid – the other day, David Beckham referred to the Premier League as "the most exposed in the world". However you interpret it, he's not wrong.

In this context, it seems almost redundant to discuss on-pitch matters, but anyway, here we are. Visiting Fratton Park is a rare pleasure these days, congestions and obstructions preferable to gangways and sightlines, authenticity and proximity to the pitch trumping whatever the newer grounds have to offer.

Ending up in row 3, my little group was afforded an excellent view of Kuszczak's silver boots and frying pan face, which grimaced every time he was forced to kick clear. Although he had probably his best game in a buttercup yellow shirt, his inability to use his feet is almost Bosnichian, and equally unacceptable.

Kicking a ball high, hard and straight is a skill learnable by anyone blessed with a working lower body, let alone a footballer. I can only surmise that the poor lad is simply too busy to squeeze in some practice.

It was disappointing to find Begovic in net for Portsmouth, with a whole half to think up insults for sanctimonious Spice Boy James that he'd have actually had to hear. Instead, the first 45 was notable for its two penalties, the ease with which Rooney converted United's bringing back dissipated annoyance for his permitting Carrick to miss at Burnley in August, though he did at least refrain from any rocking baby celebration.

The goal didn't fire United, though, who were as despicable following it as they had been before, Valencia a worthy exception despite a one-footedness so pronounced he looks like he's about to overbalance. Portsmouth also played well, the controversial penalty they were awarded a fair reflection of how the game had gone.

From row 3, it actually looked fairly clear-cut – although defenders often escape punishment when pulling shirts, Vidić didn't stay tight enough when Piquionne pulled away, making the offence too blatant to ignore. You do wonder how many more penalties will be given for similar infringements, but it doesn't alter the fact that the decision was correct and the subsequent goal the fault of the defender not the referee.

On the subject of referees, I was deeply troubled in midweek by the hair of Mark Clattenburg. Officials are there to facilitate the football in as unobtrusive a manner as possible; how, then, can we rely on someone vain enough to have implants and oblivious enough to style it like a fat man from *Soccer AM*?

The game itself ended up easier than expected, for bonus points eliciting a new excuse from good old Uncle Arry – this time the atmosphere was to blame. Although Tottenham played well early on, Kuszczak didn't make a serious save for an hour, United protecting the goal area very well despite defending very badly. After a dodgy start, Vidić grew in stature like he'd eaten a mushroom, and de Laet – pronounced to rhyme with stupid fashion-victim elbow star tatt – also did well.

On this occasion, the returning Berbatov had decided to play the role of midfield playmaker, which naturally he did rather well, even if it exacerbated the major problem with his game. Frustratingly, it ought to be solvable in a single sentence ordering him to leg it towards the box immediately after playing a defence-splitting pass, rather than amble on the spot in laconic admiration, but as yet it remains apparently unspoken.

After the game, Fergie was gushing in his praise of Anderson, and well did he deserve it. Rhapsodising the ability to run at defenders with power and pace, he unwittingly revealed an awareness of the player's best attributes that two seasons of largely withdrawn roles had suggested he was without.

Consequently, we now have the joy of a two-leg semi-final with City, a game that makes a mockery of police insistence that derbies be played at lunchtime. Unsurprisingly, beating a team that wasn't even Arsenal reserves has got them all giddy, Hughes asserting post-match that "we showed that we are a match for anybody" – typical of the baseless braggartry that comes out the mouths of liars, fantasists and blues. Followers of Ricky Hatton's career will be awaiting the inevitable turnbuckle headbutt.

Meanwhile Carlos Tévez has once again redefined magnanimity, telling us that "while I was at United, I was a loyal player" – so until you weren't, then. He also confirmed that should he score, he won't celebrate out of respect to United supporters. For the record, and regardless of the Fergie sign him up brigade, he isn't one of us, he never was, and him thinking any different winds me up. Celebrate all you like, you horrible bitter gargoyle.

Talking of City, I once again had some sympathy for Arsène Wenger this week. That it's childish and churlish to be such a bad loser is beyond doubt, but given that he is, bravo for refusing to indulge in the kind of empty gesture that infests society to such vomitous degree.

Credit to him also for giving the moralisers something different to wring their hands to, even if we still had to listen to a fair bit of Sepp Blatter's guff about the Ireland France game. The Irish request to join the tournament as a 33rd team was an act of quite astounding self-obsession, showing no regard for what FIFA acquiescing would have meant and ignoring the fact that had the handball not happened, Ireland may still have been eliminated.

FIFA, meanwhile, must hardly be able to believe the luck that's allowed them to flee the real crime – the seeding of the playoff draw – like Ronnie Biggs in an invisibility cloak. Forever playing the saviour, Blatter pledged to change the system, as "there's too much pressure".

Excuse me Sepp, but isn't that what we're here for? We follow football game after game because we're on a quest for the most feverish buzz imaginable, yet now it has to be diluted because those privileged enough to be directly involved can't handle it. Of course what Blatter really means, and later said, is that there's "too much at stake" – too much money, to be precise. Typically, this concerns no one but the suits, but Blatter is incapable of seeing beyond the end of his bespoke, which is why he's able to ignore the vicious carpetbaggers who are the true threat to the future of the game.

Portsmouth 1 v United 4 (Rooney pen 25, Rooney pen 48, Rooney 54, Giggs 87)

United: Kuszczak, Evra, Vidić, Neville, Brown, Fletcher, Valencia, Carrick (Anderson 76), Giggs, Scholes, Rooney.
Unused subs: Forster, de Laet, Park, Nani, Berbatov, Owen.

United 2 (Gibson 16, Gibson 38) **v Spurs 0**

United: Kuszczak, Neville, Brown, Vidić, de Laet, Park, Gibson, Anderson (Tošić 82), Obertan (Carrick 63), Berbatov (Macheda 63), Welbeck.
Unused subs: Amos, Owen, Giggs, Fletcher.

West Ham away 05/12/09

Wolfsburg away 08/12/09

On the Tube late one night, I couldn't help but overhear a shouted conversation between two people near me, about how ironic it was that they'd missed the previous train. Drunk and bored, I suddenly found myself interrupting to explain that this may have been annoying, but ironic it was not.

Before I knew it I was on my feet, fielding questions from the rest of the carriage and slurring my way through explanations of the dramatic, the tragic and the proleptic. Now, there's a new category to add to the list, brought to my attention by a terrace chant – once ironic, now ironically sung, "Darren Fletcher Football Genius" has added a wrinkle that we might perhaps call irony squared.

The hope is that it will be chased into the grammar books by a similar ditty – "Darron Fucking Gibson" – aired for the first time at Upton Park last Saturday. If not, it'll do as yet another example amongst the many contributions coaxed by Fergie from bit-part players; alongside the obvious names adorning the last twenty years are also those of Dublin, Cruyff, Berg and Macheda. There are numerous Vince Lombardi quotations that sum up this kind of thing, but let's go for "the only measure of who we are is what we do with what we have".

Yes, it's a good time to be Fergie right now, even if what he has is a problem of partly his own making. Brilliant in a crisis – especially one that constrains his ability to tinker – no one loves an I told you so more, and he'll doubtless be enjoying the fair few currently knocking around, a tribute to his stubbornness, judgement, and all-the-pieces-matter approach to squad building.

This has been no more in evidence than during the past week, every player stepping up to make adverse circumstances seem routine – admittedly aided by Saturday's opposition, Westairmfrewnfrew, who were compliant in the extreme. Even when Carrick was forced to replace Neville at centre-back, his injury classily jeered by the home crowd, to have avoided victory would have taken as phenomenally poor an effort as the injuries would have been excuse.

The game presented an excellent opportunity for Scholes to play himself back into form, after pre-match comments that suggested he was low on confidence – understandably so following a patchy first half of the season. For someone used not only to excelling but to giving regular masterclasses in orchestrating the whole damn thing, the gradual waning of influence must be an almost unbearable frustration, but in both games this week he showed that if used correctly, he can still make most look remedial.

That he was required to save a miserable first half reflects exceptionally badly on the efforts of those around him, United dominating possession but creating little, to flat-vowelled shouts of "they're shite, these". The second half, though, was a different story, Westairmfrewnfrew obliterated by rhythmic, patient and pacy passing. As we saw against Spurs last week and to a lesser degree at Chelsea, the 4–3–3 is a decent way of harnessing the running power of Anderson, allowing those in front of him to roam more freely at the same time. And while Gibson has only given the merest hint that he might develop into a United player, goals from midfield can cover up a lot of faults this particular formation can hide, can't they Frank.

Talking of Lampard, I must voice my disappointment that he neglected to point to the sky after last weekend's penalty miss – dear old Pat must be publicly remembered on these occasions too. That being the case, I ask that you all join me at this juncture in taking a moment to ease your fingers and eyes heavenwards. Thank you.

Clearly it's nowhere near late enough in the season to be pleased by City's consequent victory, but the reduced gap is appreciated nonetheless. Every year, the league title is awarded around now to whichever team has a built a narrow lead, the most recent winners being Chelsea, Liverpool and Arsenal. The reality is that on none of these occasions has the enthusiasm to crown champions other than United been reflective of the football I've seen, and this time, it's been shown up more quickly than usual. With both United and Chelsea now facing a hectic but favourable run of fixtures, the test will be of which squad better understands how to win. I know where my money is.

The hassle that is the matchgoing experience was put into sharper focus in midweek, with the joy of attending a game in Germany. Reasonably priced tickets, a new ground that's actually like a ground, and, most notably, no officious authority; it was possible to enjoy a beer before the game and leave when it finished, totally different to the usual European misery.

What was an annoyance was actually getting to Wolfsburg, though the time spent in the car prompted a conversation about Willie Morgan, which reminded me of the time I ran into him in a toilet. Yes, I know that sounds weird – the good news is that it gets more so. Having both had a drink or seventeen, it was only a matter of seconds before we were singing "Willie Morgan on the wing" to the very part of his anatomy with which he shares a name, before just as quickly going our separate ways.

Back to the game, United did exceptionally well to beat Wolfsburg in difficult circumstances, showing enterprise and heart. Playing midfielders in defence was actually advantageous in terms of how the team passed the ball, to the extent that I'm quite looking forward to seeing how it works against Villa this weekend.

Perhaps the most important aspect of United's win was Obertan's superb creation of goals two and three. Despite a promising start, people had already begun to question his final ball, criticism he stymied with two very different interventions – one a slaloming run followed by a composed and perfect cross, the other an intuitive, first-time through pass.

Unfortunately the beneficiary was the otherwise anonymous Owen, whose happening upon a hat-trick fooled no one. Of course the question on everybody's lips after the game was whether he'd managed to grab the match ball, and luckily good old Geoff Shreeves was on hand to ask it, Owen confiding the following response:

"I give it to the masseur to grab it – I get a bit shy when I'm holding it, as if to say 'look at me'. So I give it to the masseur and hopefully he'll get it signed for me and hopefully pop it back in my bag on the quiet when we land in Manchester".

Yes, Michael, how very self-effacing of you – hopefully no one will ever know.

West Ham 0 v United 4 (Scholes 45+1, Gibson 61, Valencia 71, Rooney 72)

United: Kuszczak, Fletcher, Neville (Carrick 33), Brown, Evra, Scholes, Valencia, Anderson, Gibson (Berbatov 67) Giggs, Rooney (Owen 82min).
Unused subs: Foster, de Laet, Nani, Park.

Wolfsburg 1 v United 3 (Owen 44, Owen 83, Owen 90+1)

United: Kuszczak, Fletcher, Carrick, Evra, Park, Gibson, Scholes, Nani (Valencia 74), Anderson, Welbeck (Obertan 74), Owen.
Unused subs: Foster, Eikrem, James, Gill, Stewart.

Villa home 12/12/09

Wolves home 15/12/09

On the way to Old Trafford as a kid, I used to stare into passing cars, wondering why not everyone was going to the game. You're in Manchester, United are playing, and you're quite clearly not busy – what else is to do?

The answer, of course, is nothing, but the takeover and resultant price hikes have since forced people to stay away on principle – perhaps the Glazers were actually funded by a consortium of fed-up wives. Anyway, the upshot is that games, particularly those like Tuesday's at home to Wolves, no longer sell out, leaving season ticket holders stuck at work with nothing better to do with their seats than give them to the likes of me.

It'd be wrong to say that there aren't advantages to boycotting – less awayday guilt, less hassle, less expense and less general despair – but not having been to Old Trafford for a while, I was glad of the opportunity. Despite it all, there's still nowhere like it, even on the dullest of dull nights (and this one was duller).

But first things first, and to last weekend's game against Villa, easily the toughest until we play Arsenal at the end of January. You might, therefore, have thought – particularly given the injury situation – that the strongest available team would be selected. Well you might have done had Fergie not been involved.

It appears that three useless cup displays does a league start win, Park's selection agonising evidence of a team picked according to rota rather than form. Recently, it's looked like 4–3–3 is the best way of exploiting its strengths and hiding its weaknesses – bad news for Berbatov – but even in a 4–4–2, and particularly without a prolific centre-forward, the wide attackers must be a genuine goal threat. Park, however, rarely scores or creates, buzzing around like a mosquito with balance issues and only slightly more usefully; in a United career that began four and a half years ago, he's managed twelve goals, whilst the far-from-perfect, far-from-prolific Antonio Valenthia already has five.

Even so, United enjoyed enough possession and created enough chances to have won comfortably, though you could just as easily argue that Villa merited their victory for taking one of theirs and defending it well. That said, crediting them with a performance of verve and wit is overdoing it; the goal came very much out of the blue, following a period of sustained assault, and the second half saw them massed in their own half like pawns on a chessboard.

Although the blame for the defeat rests with the players, they were certainly not helped by the management. In the first half, Rooney was easily United's most dangerous player, but after the break was withdrawn into a deeper role to facilitate the arrival of Owen. This was not particularly helpful, as for now, Rooney's best as a centre-forward, with only one man blocking his route to goal – his passing isn't precise enough to dissect entire defences. With Villa condensing the game well, what was needed was pace out wide, but instead we got Berbatov, who in doing quite well also added to the clutter; only in the final few moments should weight of numbers take precedence over shape.

If that game was a let down, midweek against Wolves was more a non-event than any football match I can remember attending. This was due in part to circumstance – the handball that led to the penalty couldn't be seen from most parts of the ground, so there was neither appeal nor roar on its award – and similar reaction greeted the second goal, the ball sneaking over the line after appearing to have been saved.

There's already been plenty said about the eleven Mick McCarthy sent out, so just two more things. One: they're not much cop at football, but I'd love to see Maierhofer and Elokobi on opposite sides of the octagon; and two: if times were hard, you could make Greg Halford's shirt by cutting arm holes in a Halfords bag.

A proper football club with a rich history, you'd expect that Wolves fans would boast a repertoire extending beyond the generic relegation songs sung by all the other teams we only play every few seasons, but that's absolutely not so. Not that United were much better; suddenly presented with a player who can score from outside the box, the cries of "shooooot" each time Gibson got the ball were lame enough to make you wish he'd never encouraged them in the first place.

Elsewhere, Ryan Giggs was named BBC's Sports Personality of the Year this week – impossible to defend in a rare year of legitimate contenders. Still, it was hard not to feel vicarious warmth at his success, his longevity the reward for the dedicated way in which he looks after himself – in a recent interview with *The Times*, Giggs confided that "after a slice of buttered toast, I feel less mentally sharp". Apparently Nani usually has his share.

Talking of missing mental sharpness, it's been another bad week for the mickey mousers. With attempts to sound rousing heightened by the 50th anniversary of Bill Shankly's appointment, let's enjoy remembering that when he was offered the manager's job by then-Liverpool chairman Tom Williams, the conversation went something like this:

Williams: How would you like to manage the best club in the world?

Shankly: Why, is Matt Busby packing it in?

And thanks again to Jamie Carragher, who this week treated us to the following:

"Between now and May it's going to be a grind at times but we've got to stick together, get through it and, as I'm doing, pray to God that at the end of the season there will be something worthwhile for what we've gone through."

Jamie, I'm sure there's a spot in heaven reserved especially for you, and well does your suffering deserve it. Perhaps you should change your name to Job.

This particular bout of stoic misery came after Arsenal easily overturned a half-time deficit, apparently inspired by Wenger's dressing room screaming; how very scary that must be. As a general rule, there's not much funnier than anger, but that must have got lips a-twisting and teeth a-tongue-biting like nothing since Biggus Dickus.

For all his whinging, bad hair, and poor syntax, I have time for Wenger, famously incorruptible and one of few who genuinely seems to care about the game. However in threatening to sue the Dutch FA following Robin van Persie's injury, he's putting his own interests above the greater good; if he won, then international football might be irreparably damaged – fine with me, and better for him, but the majority seem quite taken with it.

Having been forced into selling players against his will as a consequence of the Bosman ruling, Wenger should know that just because the law permits something, it doesn't mean it's for the best – and if that isn't proof enough, he should consider the Mancunian cars no longer driving to Old Trafford.

United 0 v Villa 1

United: Kuszczak, Fletcher, Brown, Vidić, Evra, Carrick, Anderson (Gibson 68), Valencia, Giggs (Owen 46), Park (Berbatov), Rooney. Unused subs: Foster, de Laet, Obertan, Welbeck.

United 3 (Rooney pen 30, Vidić 43, Valencia 66) v Wolves 0

United: Kuszczak, de Laet, Carrick, Vidić (Fletcher 60), Evra, Valencia, Gibson, Scholes, Obertan (Welbeck 71), Berbatov, Rooney (Owen 76). Unused subs: Foster, Fábio, Anderson, Park.

Fulham away 19/12/09

Oscar Wilde once joked that he was so clever, often he didn't understand a word of what he was saying, and he wasn't even speaking in Scottish. So imagine how hard it must be for poor Fergie to decode his complexities into a suitable football team; seeing something that others can't might be a hallmark of genius, but there's always the chance that you're just seeing things.

Because football is a perfectly balanced game, its formations are an unsolvable riddle; add something in one place, lose something in another. Nonetheless, there's a reason no one plays 3–5–2 anymore, and why its most famous proponent also thinks that suffering is a punishment for sins in a previous life. But for some hallucinatory reason, Fergie decided it was the best way of lining up at Fulham, forcing players already in unfamiliar roles into an unfamiliar system – one that effectively ignores the four corners of the pitch, particularly disadvantageous for a team that aims to make the playing space as wide as possible.

With a squad shorn of defenders, not even the most inveterate of acid casualties would have deployed one of its best at wing-back, but there Patrice Evra was, not even moved when things went wrong. Meanwhile, Darren Fletcher, whose drive in midfield was so sorely missed against Villa, toiled at the back to no avail.

According to the law of moments, an object is in equilibrium when the net force and net torque exerted upon it are zero. Unfortunately, at the very time he needs to do least, Fergie is pressing and twisting like a bodybuilding Vulcan, conned into believing his own omnipotence after getting away with it against West Ham and Wolfsburg.

In fact the Wolfsburg game was a triple punishment, resulting in yet another tedious trip to Milan instead of one to Seville, as well as encouraging continued perseverance with the frankly execrable Michael Owen, about whom Fergie seems determined to be proved right. Notwithstanding the obvious exception, after which he should have been summarily binned on the basis that it could only get worse, he has contributed startlingly little, and not even for a single moment looked a footballer of United quality.

Although this continued at Fulham, he was in no way helped by the incompetence of those around him. Watching the highlights, I was no less shocked to hear the commentator say "and Scholes has lost the ball again" than I was observing it at the time, despite his waning powers. The last two games have also illustrated how important Giggs continues to be, though he claimed this week not to have noticed much difference since Ronaldo left; he must be eating more buttered toast than he's letting on.

Anyway, once Fulham scored, the game was effectively over – there was more chance of Godot turning up than a United goal. Expecting to see the players coming out for the second half dripping with tea and hoping that Fergie and Phelan had also chucked a few cups at each other, they instead trooped meekly out to immediately concede again – you can only hope that the tanning machine recently reported to reside at Carrington does actually hand out tannings.

Whilst even the grizzliest car crash is strangely compelling, its footballing equivalent was anything but, United's show bereft of any redeeming quality whatsoever, other than the fact that it ended. All those involved should feel very ashamed indeed.

Luckily no one else has been good enough to take proper advantage, and though neither Chelsea nor Arsenal are mugs (or should that be mags?), it's fair to say that this year's champions will be the weakest in a while, whoever they turn out to be. Talking of Arsenal, their substitutes showed no shame in sitting on the bench at Hull wrapped in blankets, only marginally better than the furry animal outfits they're pictured in all over London; I wonder why opponents consider them such a soft touch.

Of course the principal joy of this time of the year is the PDC Darts World Championship, and we have number three seed James Wade to thank for furnishing us with the following anecdote, in an interview with the *Daily Star*:

"I was down in the local chemist in Cobham and this guy went to me, 'All right, Wadey?' I thought it was someone trying to be a pest. I replied, 'All right'. He then texted my girlfriend with the message: 'How rude is your boyfriend?'"

"He" turned out to be John Terry, so please be forewarned: should he ever deign to greet you, be sure to respond with requisite ecstasy.

Terry was one of many players to turn down the ludicrously acquired coin of Manchester City, who this week dispensed with the services of poor old Leslie Hughes.

It's sad that ten years of genuine heroism can be irreparably tarnished by an 18–month period, but it's fair to say that most United supporters will never look at him in the same way again; not just for going there, but because of the alacrity with which he embraced their every aspect.

He may have been unlucky to lose his job, but knew what he was getting himself into and deserves criticism for the total lack of imagination in any of his signings. At first it seemed odd that Roberto Mancini was considered to be a definitively better option, his success in Italy predicated on the disqualification of the opposition, but then that's exactly what City are attempting, just by way of artificially-gained wealth.

And we must also be pleased Hughes failed so that we were not denied the breathtakingly mendacious arrogance of Garry Cook's press conference. Justifiably nailed for precisely that by most sensible commentators, there has been insufficient chortling at his utter dislocation from reality, so do please enjoy the following highlights:

He began by pontificating that "the owner, chairman and myself all worked to give Mark any resources he required", but did not expand on his contribution to the exchequer of the Al Nahyan family; no doubt without him they'd all be living in a Baniyas slum.

Cook then went on to claim that the club was "like any other business", before using almost every cliché in the book with which adults patronise children; I was almost expecting him to accuse the press of showing off to its friends due to overtiredness. After talking of "a process of change that we've all had to go through", he then majored on his "disappointment" – as though this was somehow chastising to one and all – before asserting that the matter was closed, simply because he said it was.

And even then, he wasn't done:

"What has made this club very angry is the misinterpretation of our statement. We are so incensed by the misinterpretation that we plan to re-issue the statement again [sic]".

Issue the statement again? By jove what fury! World be warned: mess with City at your peril.

Fulham 3 v United 0

United: Kuszczak, Fletcher, de Laet (Fábio 58), Carrick, Evra, Valencia, Scholes, Anderson, Gibson (Berbatov 58), Owen (Welbeck 72), Rooney. Unused subs: Foster, Park, Obertan, Tošić.

Hull away 27/12/09

Wigan home 30/12/09

Where to find happiness is a question that has vexed mankind since God was a foetus; for some it's in a warm gun, others a cigar called Hamlet, and for an unfortunate few, nowhere at all. That being the case, we're duty-bound to gorge on it any time it happens to turn up, because we've got no idea when we'll come across it next.

And that's where football comes in, supplying us with a weekly thrill and legitimate reason to celebrate success; if glorying in personal achievement is only vanity in disguise, then true joy comes about through the achievements of others.

Second only to being a parent – the ultimate in vicarious delight – supporting a football team is of similar genus, the ability to claim ownership but not credit making it ok to enjoy things when they go right; the keenness of supporters to call players "son", "lad" and "kid" is no coincidence. It's unclear as to at what age this becomes unridiculous – at 30, I'm still too young – but it's impossible not to feel paternal towards the two bouncing bundles of curls and puppy fat otherwise known as the da Silva twins.

There's simply nothing about them that doesn't make me smile: the notion of twins playing for United, the joy in their joy, the way that they play. There was even something loveable about Rafael's inept attempt to conceal his guilt after impetuously gifting Hull a penalty last weekend, as though denying to his mother that he'd snaffled her last slice of bolo.

Of course it helped that the resultant equaliser mattered less because he'd managed to spark the team into life at the end of a largely abominable first half effort, his enterprise driving a period of pressure that culminated in the opening goal. In the event, Hull drawing level actually did United a favour, forcing some urgency and tempo into their play, even if there were still far too many long balls belted at no one in particular. Consequently, the introduction of Park helped matters, the team profiting from his excellent movement without ruining it by giving him the ball.

Despite years of watching terrible teams suddenly improve when confronted by United, I was still surprised by how well Hull played, and there are plenty of others I'd prefer to see relegated. Phil Bronze may be a self-important cheesemeister, but following the on-pitch berating of his players – a rare acknowledgement of their accountability to supporters – it'll take more than an earpiece and some hair gel to make him as dislikeable as some. It was also nice to see a ground with so many kids in it, even if it's far too big for the number of people it holds, and outside it, I was amused to see a fat hairy dog dressed in full Hull kit (insert gag here).

Anyway, midweek against Wigan was a far less stressful affair, United setting about their opponents in appropriate fashion from the off. Suitable punishment for Martinez's mouth earlier in the season, it was also richly deserved by whoever decided that preventing United from kicking towards the Stretford End in the second half would make any difference to the outcome.

It's no coincidence that Valencia's best performance so far came with an attacking threat behind him – I imagine he'll be as dismayed as I wasn't to learn that John O'Shea may be missing for a further two months. Rafael's propensity to remedy positional errors with immediate fouls will cost the occasional goal, but he needs games not protection.

As was the case with United at Fulham, it's hard to read much into the performance of one side when the other was so poor, however much they were made to look so. Nonetheless, it was encouraging to see Rooney behaving in the manner of a proper centre-forward, stealing across his man at the near post for the first goal and trying to steal the second from Carrick. Now he just needs to score some headers.

With the game not on telly, it was another that had to be viewed on the laptop, this time accompanied by the realisation that I'd never before watched United from the toilet. I admit to being disproportionately overjoyed by this discovery, far more than I was on discovering my addiction to following the inane inanities of the imbecilic imbeciles posting their comments on the site. OMG!!!! MANU5–0 LOL LOL LOLS!!!!!!! indeed.

Force-fed a diet of boring cup draws over the last few years, the next few days provide the rare treat of ties against Leeds and City. There's some amusement to be had in beating both with reserve sides, but I imagine most would rather see a few first-teamers involved – opportunities to give the former a well-deserved hiding are rare these days, as are those to take direct responsibility for adding another year to the Stretford End ticker.

That said, City may win the league. Well Mancini thinks so anyway; it appears to have taken all of a week for him to be fully indoctrinated into the cult of the Blue Moonies. Their fans, meanwhile, have been similarly duped in their usual way, the manager's scarf apparently suggesting Italian sophistication rather than badge-kissing tokenism garnished with symbolic noose. One thing we know for sure, though, is that Mancini must have a mighty fine larder of garibaldis, otherwise he'd have been forced to make do with Real Madrid, like Kaká.

Finally for this week, Arsène Wenger's suggestion that kick-ins be introduced into the game. The long throw, apparently, is "an unfair advantage", albeit one easily remedied by not buying small defenders and indulging dodgy goalkeepers, he didn't go on to say. Wenger frequently criticises opposition teams for their temerity in not playing in the exact way that would make them easiest to beat – this is but another example – and naturally it's the game's fault.

One of the beauties of football is the way its laws permit inferior outfits to compete with those more technically adept, and forever must it remain so; if the better team always won, we'd be demanding an awful lot from those guns and cigars.

Hull 1 v United 3 (Rooney 45+2, Dawson o.g. 73, Berbatov 82)

United: Kuszczak, Rafael, Vidić, Brown, Evra, Valencia (Park 64), Carrick, Fletcher, Giggs (Obertan 78), Berbatov, Rooney.
Unsed subs: Foster, Owen, Welbeck, Fábio, de Laet.

United 5 (Rooney 28, Carrick 32, Rafael 45, Berbatov 50, Valencia 75) **v Wigan 0**

United: Kuszczak, Rafael, Vidić (Anderson 68), Brown, Evra (Fábio 68), Valencia, Fletcher, Carrick, Park, Berbatov (Welbeck 68), Rooney.
Unused subs: Amos, Neville, Owen, Obertan.

Leeds home 03/01/10

When Morrissey declared that he had forgiven Jesus, he was criticised by some for daring to suggest that could possibly be necessary. In similar vein, there'll doubtless be plenty who'll criticise me when I say that I haven't, and will never, forgive Fergie.

Even though I've spoken them hundreds of times over the last four years, these are words that never flow easily. When the bible is read in synagogues, it's sung according to a melody known as the trup, with each word marked by a particular note – one of which, the *shalshelet*, appears only five times in the entire Torah. It's use is to indicate a pause, whilst its subject suffers the agonising turmoil of what's termed a sin against the soul – when Joseph rejects the advances of Potiphar's outrageously attractive wife, for example. And that's how it feels to despise the man responsible for a reality so inconceivable that even Joseph himself couldn't have dreamt it.

That heroes always let you down is a cliché for a reason, but even so, you'd have thought that Fergie had racked up sufficient credit to remain one forever. Although Busby status became unobtainable following unsued-upon allegations made in two BBC documentaries – the first based on a biography written by eminent United historian Michael Crick, the second a similarly authoritiative investigation into his agent son Jason – the reported indiscretions are dwarfed by achievements that won him significant slack. However his ushering in of the takeover reeled it all in and then some, imperilling the club in a way that was not only unacceptable but entirely avoidable.

Rewind to early 2005 and things looked a little different, even though horse semen and money appeared to have become more important than the famous Man United – evidenced not just through the dispute over Rock of Gibraltar, but the disgusting signings and performances that defined the period. Yet even then, and as the song goes, every single one of us still loved Alex Ferguson; not as blindly as before, but nonetheless with devotion. A hefty part of the reason why was the following quotation, dated November 2004:

"There's a stronger rapport between the club and the fans than there's ever been. We are both of a common denominator; we don't want the club to be in anyone else's hands. That is the way that the club stands with that. I support that."

Fairly categorical, you might think, and indeed it was, until it wasn't. Some might say that Fergie had no choice but to renege on his word because his job became dependent on it, but I'm not having that; had he clearly stated a refusal to work with the Glazers, the banks would never have lent them the money. But at the same time, he'd have known that the Glazers needed him more than the plc, so stayed silent to protect his own position, already more heavily fortified than a man with a hip flask full of malt and a packet full of Nik Naks. And supporters have been paying for it, financially and emotionally, ever since.

Yes, there's plenty the authorities could have done, and yes, David Gill could have kept his word too, but we never expected we could rely on them. Fergie, on the other hand, was one of us, the proudly socialist man of the people who promised never to forget his roots, nor the backing he was given by United's support in his ridiculous dispute with Coolmore.

Fast forward a few months to August 2005, and United were in Budapest to play Debrecen. Happening upon the official party at the airport, a disgruntled fan took issue with Fergie over the takeover. The club's official website reports that the following was said:

Fan: "You've fucked us over too, you could've spoken out about it."
Sir Alex: "I've got close friends who've been working with me here for 15 years. They come first in all of this."
Fan: "So don't the fans come first?"
Fergie: "Well I suppose they do come somewhere."
Fan: "You what? That's well out of order."
Sir Alex: "If you don't like it, go and watch Chelsea."
Fan: "The fans have been screwed right over. It costs me over £20 a game as it is."
Sir Alex: "It costs more than that at Chelsea – go and watch them."

In one short conversation, a legacy two decades in the building, not just tarnished, but forever buried under a mountain of turds. Despite the pompous pontifications in his autobiography, to Fergie football is evidently not about more than on-pitch accomplishment; identity, community and belonging are insignificant when compared to the needs of his little fraternity, which the cynical might claim is comprised of but one person.

So it is that blame for anything going wrong can be legitimately attributed to him. Lose at home to Leeds? Well if Fergie had spoken out, you can be sure there'd have been a better striker on the bench than Michael Owen, who has missed a quite remarkable number of chances since he began infesting the club with his presence. This week, Owen was advised that to galvanise his career, he should address matters of feng shui, by Geoff Boycott of all people – not exactly renowned for the lightness of his touch, shall we say. Anyway, though I can't comment about the positioning of the furniture in Owen's mansion, United's squad would certainly look more centred and aesthetic without him in it.

Notwithstanding Fergie's duplicity, the eleven he selected ought to have been more than capable of disposing of Dirty Leeds, well though they played. Vidić pulling out in the warm up wasn't helpful – according to the ever-insightful Mike Phelan, "there was something wrong with his body" – but it was reasonable to expect better from Wes Brown, who endured one of the periodic nightmares that reminded everyone why he was displaced by Vidić in the first place.

Talking of Phelan, one can only wonder how on earth he has risen to become Fergie's number two (and yes, there's a childish joke there). With the manager an infrequent training ground presence, and renowned neither as coach nor tactician, it would be handy if the person charged with so doing was properly qualified, rather than happening to be around when the previous incumbent left. Carlos Queiroz certainly wasn't anyone's favourite, often blamed for an unnecessarily conservative approach, but at least while he was around, the team defended properly, and it's hard to think of any players who've improved significantly since he left.

Perhaps the major difference between this United squad and those of recent years is the number of players able to make the crucial difference when things aren't going well. This season, only Berbatov, Giggs and Rooney have proved themselves in that category, whereas in the past, there've been a few on the pitch, with a few more waiting on the bench. It's now twice that chasing a goal, Gibson has either been left on or brought on in forlorn hope that he belts one in from distance, the kind of quiet desperation that is really not the United way.

All in all, there've been better weeks to be a Red – with the press finally noticing what anyone with a brain could see in 2005, reminders of the of the debt and the future it promises are everywhere. Luckily, amusement lurks in the usual places, so thanks more than ever to Jamie Carragher and Manchester City. The former, interviewed following Liverpool's draw with Reading came up with this:

"I've been to Cardiff a few times but I'd love to get to Wembley. My son is six or seven years old and I'd love to take him to Wembley to watch Liverpool".

Not having kids, I confess to being slightly out of my element here, but after conducting a straw poll amongst friends who do, I can reveal that not a single one was stumped by the age of their offspring.

Meanwhile, now that City's buy-all-the-domestic-players-not-good-enough-for-the-best-teams plan has failed, they're going down the buy-once-great-but-now-hasbeens route. Rejected by Juan Sebastián Verón, despite Mancini informing us that "all the players want to join Manchester City", instead they've signed Patrick Vieira, who didn't even offer the usual massive club bluster, simply admitting that he needs first-team football if he's to play in the World Cup. No doubt when this policy doesn't work either, it'll be followed by the buy-anyone-young-who-once-had-a-good-game approach.

Still, with the money that City now have, a trophy of some sort will probably arrive at some point, but even when it does, it'll be utterly meaningless. There's a difference between wealth a club has earned on its own merits, and wealth it's been donated like some sort of charity case; it renders any subsequent success as plastic as Eastlands' famous empty seats. And for anyone pointing out that United now have those too, you know exactly who to blame.

United 0 v Leeds 1

United: *Kuszczak, Neville, Brown, Evans, Fábio, Obertan (Giggs 57), Gibson, Anderson (Owen 69), Welbeck (Valencia 57), Berbatov, Rooney. Unused subs: Amos, Rafael, Carrick, Tošić.*

Birmingham away 09/01/10

Football may be the ultimate in communal communion, but if that were all it was, it wouldn't be what it is. Each of us has a relationship with our team that anchors it in our personal history, a combination of little details and significant events that tell us who we are and what we want to be.

For me, the former is founded on the fact that Old Trafford is the only place frequented both by me and a grandfather I never met, the latter most obviously connected to an evening 15 years ago this month, when, as a teenager trying to work myself out, I went to Selhurst Park and saw Eric Cantona do his thing. In a moment that felt like it'd been specifically designed with me in mind, the duty to be true to oneself in every circumstance was laid bare, and internalised forever.

So when people damage United, I take it personally, which is why I'm so militant in my hatred of the Glazers. And suddenly, no one's telling me that it's misplaced; I told you so has never sounded as mortifying.

With the owners seeking to refinance their loans by way of a bond issue – and seeing it advertised in Monday's *FT* was a bit like finding the Queen begging on a street corner – the law insists that they provide full details of the club's financial position, revealing for the first time the true horror of United's predicament. Now that I've disinfected my eyeballs, this is what we've learnt:

Cash is required very, very badly; as Roy Walker might say, it's time for the Ready Money Round. Despite winning a third consecutive league title and reaching a second successive European Cup final, were it not for the sale of Ronaldo, United would have operated at a loss during the last year; even if the player had wanted to stay, the debt would have insisted he be sold anyway.

In similar vein, though the new sponsorship deal with Aon doesn't begin until the summer, £36 million of the £80 million fee has already been drawn down – and not to provide Fergie with the funds to strengthen the squad, though the prospectus acknowledges that continued on-pitch success is essential. However £22.9 million *has* been paid out in "loans" and "management fees" – or in other words, for make benefit great nation of Glazerstan. Not only are supporters funding their ownership of the club, but their lifestyle too.

Plans are also outlined for the sale and leaseback of United's training ground or, as the prospectus calls it, the "Carrington Transaction". Mooted as simply a possibility, that it's a defined term tells you it's near enough a certainty, and once the bond deal is done, will be completed faster than you can say Malcolm Glazer – and certainly faster than he can say it. In an act of stunningly legal larceny, the family will transfer ownership of the complex from United to one of their other companies, mortgage it, and then charge the club rent for the privilege of its use. The funds from this new revenue stream can then be directed towards the PIK loans – debt for which the Glazers are personally liable – or to pay down the senior debt that's secured against the assets of the club. Were they to settle on the second option, the "Old Trafford Transaction" becomes little more than a matter of time.

But really, I'm an overreacting no-nothing crank. There's no gain for the Glazers in running United into the ground, and Fergie says everything's ok, so it must be, right?

In the circumstances, talking about the part of football that's only a game seems ridiculous, despite the nauseous reality that this season is as good as it's likely to get for some time. I'd hoped that we'd manage to inveigle a 19th title to sustain us through the upcoming lean period, but for the first time in a while, it looks like it may be beyond us; how very lucky that Liverpool chose last season rather than this to string a few results together.

It isn't even that the squad isn't good enough – the miserable quality of the best sides in the division means that this one could get the job done – but it's no longer good enough to win whoever happens to be picked, and 101 games have now passed since the same eleven started consecutive games. Fergie, for reasons known to himself alone, finds this both clever and amusing, but then he also thinks that United's first half display against Birmingham was "brilliant".

They did start like they meant it, but as has happened almost every time they've come up against a well-organised team, and despite the pretty possession, scoring has been a problem. The configuration of the team didn't help, but this was more an issue of intention than formation; 4–5–1 isn't conservative per se, but demands attacking midfielders and proper wingers.

Instead, we got a central triumvirate with five goals and four assists between them so far this season, along with Park who has neither of either. Presumably selected for the purported defensive abilities that were unsurprisingly absent in the joke that was Birmingham's goal, it provided sure evidence that United had come to win 1–0, augmented by his replacement with Giggs when a winning goal was required. That he was introduced to play from the right with Valencia on the left was baffling, stationing two of the most one-footed players I've ever seen on the wrong sides, thus narrowing a pitch that needed the opposite. An honourable mention to Valencia nonetheless, who battled hard and has stood out over the last month or so – too bad that he's not good enough to get it done on his own.

As United chased the game, what was most frustratingly evident was the extent to which they missed van der Sar. With one midfielder sent off and another substituted, they had less of the ball than usual, so needed to make the most of it once they got it. But each time a Birmingham attack broke down, Kuszczak was capable only of belting it out of play or straight back to them, and at no point was there a feeling of impending goal.

Perhaps the most notable episode of the afternoon came at half-time, a sudden outbreak of police thuggery that received not a single column inch of coverage – unlike the complete non-event that was Barnsley Baltigate. With five minutes to go until the restart, things were proceeding as normal – general disorderliness, no hint of trouble – when from nowhere, a mob of police in full riot gear appeared, shoving anyone in their way and forming a line down the middle of the concourse.

A crowd of around 200 massed around them, and some beer was thrown – commonplace, regardless of whether police are there or not, as anyone whose job it is to know should have known – at which point a goodly portion of the officers on duty began whacking anyone who had the misfortune to be pushed into them. Several appeared to have misunderstood the meaning of the word "shield" – one in particular used his to knock someone to the ground as he walked on by, then kicking him twice as he lay prone on the floor. Others preferred their cute little mini-batons, leaving some bleeding profusely from head wounds – again, not those seeking a fight.

A chat with the Football Supporters Federation revealed that supporters of both West Ham and Chelsea have reported problems with West Midlands Police in recent weeks, some of whose number were as incredulous as I was as to what was going on; had they not been there, no trouble would have ensued, and had they left when it started to go wrong, things would have quietened immediately. Instead, they escalated matters by calling for reinforcements, some visibly delighted to be involved.

Although I'm thankful to them for facilitating a brilliant goon and tumble down the stairs when the United goal went in – restoring some faith in a match-going experience that had taken yet another hit pre-match when someone complained to me that he'd been unable to wash his hands after using the toilet – it'd be nice to know what it was all about, as it would be for those involved to be suitably punished.

If there was little cheer around this week, there's still plenty of scope for things to get worse; whatever happens at home to Burnley, a midweek defeat to City would be unpleasantness incarnate. The players owe us a performance in that one, not just because they lost to Leeds, but for tempering the heartiness with which we can guffaw at Liverpool. That said, even the most intense laughter wouldn't have made things very much better – as City fans are painfully aware, defining your existence by the failings of others is no existence at all.

Birmingham 1 v United 1 (Dann o.g. 63)

United: Kuszczak, Rafael, Brown, Evans, Evra, Carrick, Scholes
(Diouf 81), Valencia, Fletcher, Park (Giggs 65), Rooney.
Unused subs: Amos, Neville, Fábio, Anderson, Owen.
Sent off: Fletcher.

Burnley home 16/01/10
city away 19/01/10

Many a 90s schoolkid will be familiar with the Guns n' Roses song *Get In The Ring*, the aggressive anger and swearing that appears towards its end a guaranteed parent-riler when played at the appropriate volume. But despite luxuriating in the vitriol, I never did agree with its opening couplet, which goes as follows:

"Why do you look at me when you hate me? Why should I look at you when you make me hate you too".

There's little as invigoratingly life-affirming as hatred, and I was disappointed in Axl for trying to ignore it; clearly he'd never heard of Manchester City (funny that). I've always felt that hatred should be hard to come by, but with City you have the paradox of them making it so easy that it forces you to hate them even more for ruining the challenge. And boy oh boy, how unfeasibly easy they do make it.

Let's start with the idiot in charge of the PA who refers to the players by their first names – as though they're everybody's personal friend, rather than a collection of hired mercenaries unwanted by anyone bigger and better. And if that toadying's not enough, try the banner that hangs in the stadium – not ground – that they conned the council into paying for, in the face of definitive academic evidence that Manchester is red (thank you Dr Adam Brown of Manchester Institute for Popular Culture, Manchester Metropolitan University). Anyway, it reads "Manchester thanks you Sheikh Mansour", alongside words in Arabic that presumably mean exactly the same.

Why are both languages required? Because it's part of the same ostentation that has Garry Cook "working" in an Eastlands room with the blinds up at the precise time that he can be seen by people arriving for the match.

But what extreme magnanimity it is to offer thanks to the man who purchased their heritage as an ego massaging, country-aggrandising toy, a magnanimity also on display – like everything else they do – in the minute's silence they held following the tragic events in Cabinda. No doubt this heartfelt gesture helped Emmanuel Adebayor feel very much better, the sympathy so sincere that within a few days they were lambasting him for being interviewed wearing an Arsenal polo shirt. Then, but a week later, you have row upon row of cravenly bitter imbeciles literally falling over themselves to point out the hilarity of the Munich air crash. Well, they do say that you need a sense of humour to be a blue.

Tuesday's game was City's first semi in 29 years, and perusing the badly-dressed deformities that were everywhere you looked, it wasn't hard to see why. Choosing to mark the occasion by dimming the lights pre-match, adding to the circus feel, they unwittingly aided the creation of a more suitable atmosphere by drawing even more attention to the red flares that illuminated the United end. These were then utterly usurped by a punk version of Blue Moon that was authentic, inspiring, and classy.

The first half was fairly similar to that of the season's first derby, United carelessly allowing City back into the game after going ahead. Even so, they still needed the benefit of a poor decision to score, Rafael unlucky to concede a penalty for a perfectly-timed foul on the edge of the box.

Refereeing errors are generally understandable and not worthy of complaint, but this one grated more than most. Although not pressed into making a decision, Mike Dean nonetheless seized the opportunity to show off his cleverness in having spotted that which had escaped those less sharp-eyed than he.

There are certain officials whose demeanour makes it easy to understand why players become so enraged, and Dean is one, gesticulating at them whilst looking the other way like a primary school teaching traffic warden. But then what's to expect from a man who comes from Wirral and sings *You'll Never Walk Alone* after a few drinks?

That isn't to say Dean was responsible for the result, even if he didn't help, also incorrectly awarding City the corner that resulted in the second goal. Seldom threatening in open play, almost every set-piece created minor panic, particularly infuriating given the poverty of United's – even after 20 years, Giggs is still botching them with ball-aching regularity.

Partly due to a team changed more often than Style Council's moods, partly due to the make up of the midfield, for all their territorial dominance, United mustered very few chances. A trio of Fletcher, Anderson and Carrick simply doesn't offer sufficient attacking threat, as we saw in the Chelsea game; if the formation is to work properly, it can bear only two of them, along with either Giggs or Scholes.

What it can do without is Carrick, in whom I've finally lost patience; a good player, but not good enough often enough when it's required the most. The sale of Saha robbed him of the pace up front that exploits his ability to spot an early pass, but that's nowhere near sufficient excuse for his regular insipidity.

So as is now regular, United monopolised possession with a grim, ponderous turgidity that would make AS Byatt proud, constantly stumped by what to do around the area that Subbuteo veterans will know as the shooting line. Simply by virtue of being another body, the introduction of Owen improved matters, weleasing Wooney, and his combination play with Giggs and Evra down United's left was the most likely source of an equaliser.

Scholes's belated arrival also helped. Although it's now impossible to predict when he'll control a game from the start, his ability to come on and move the ball cleverly and quickly highlights the deficiencies of those initially charged with the task, the round-the-corner pass to Rooney no longer the only alternative to knocking it wide.

And so to Carlos Tévez. It was obvious when he left that he'd score against United, and judging by his celebrations, he was preoccupied with showing how much being kicked out stung, rather than sharing the moment with his new temporary friends. This was partly a reaction to things said by Gary Neville, who then capped a week of oblivious self-embarrassment by lamely swearing in response. The FA, apparently, are "investigating", whatever that means; looking at a picture hardly requires the sleuthing skills of Philip Marlowe. It'd be refreshing if they censured him for using the single-fingered salute of a teenage American girl, but you can't rely on anyone to maintain standards these days.

This episode of idiocy was preceded a few days earlier by some comments relating to the debt, on which Neville offered the following helpful insight:

"We're always very well protected and we never get involved in the financial side of things… as players we never get involved in those things; our job is purely on the pitch and we allow people who are paid to do jobs in other areas of the club to do their job. It's nothing to do with us at all."

What a relief! The players are well protected! Well, Gary, you horrible, selfish little man, I'm glad that you're alright, and that you consider United's ruination to be none of your business. I never thought I'd find myself deferring to Tévez's turn of phrase, but "boot-licking moron" is pretty much perfect.

It isn't that we ever expected any help from the players who, Solskjaer and Cantona apart, have sauntered along as though there's nothing amiss. But the least they can do is keep their fucking mouths shut.

Perhaps this week's starkest reminder of the liability came during Satuday's game against Burnley, when, in a double substitution, the numbers 7 and 32 were introduced. A year ago that would have meant Ronaldo and Tévez, but it now signifies Owen, and, as Fergie calls him, "the boy Mame Diouf". Pleasingly, the former had a perfect view of the latter scoring his first United goal, his inability to force any semblance of a smile precisely indicative of the attitude that has endeared him to no one.

Talking of endearing people, John Terry appeared back on the radar the other day, discussing the toilet habits that are but a single fascinating facet of this fascinating man. Of course we already know a bit about these particular peccadilloes from his public cup-urination trick, but must nonetheless be grateful to him for filling another hole in our knowledge; apparently he always uses the same dressing room stone:

"For some reason I could only go there. And the foreign lads don't really get why I'm waiting behind them when there's plenty of spaces elsewhere!"

Yes, such stage fright must be totally incomprehensible to those teammates born outside the UK, particularly the ones who suffered for it in Moscow. I wonder if they can bring themselves to look at him.

United 3 (Berbatov 64, Rooney 69, Diouf 90+1) **v Burnley 0**

United: *van der Sar, Neville, Brown, Evans, Evra, Valencia, Carrick (Anderson 66), Scholes, Nani, Berbatov (Owen 73), Rooney (Diouf 74). Unused subs: Kuszczak, Fábio, Rafael, Park.*

city 2 v United 1 (Giggs 17)

United: *van der Sar, Rafael (Diouf 90), Brown, Evans, Evra, Valencia (Scholes 88), Carrick, Fletcher, Giggs, Anderson (Owen 72), Rooney. Unused Subs: Kuszczak, Neville, Fábio, Park.*

Hull home 23/01/10

city home 27/01/10

The delicious thing about perfection is that it's only perfect until it's perfected. So for a few short months, it was thought that winning a league derby in injury time was as good as this season could possibly get, but, joyously, we were mistaken. O frabjous day! Callooh! Callay!

This time, the beauty was how many times City must've thought they'd escaped; after Rooney's miss, after Tévez's equaliser, after Carrick's miss, after Given's save. But no they had not, not by a long chalk – rather like Matthias, son of Deuteronomy of Gath, they were only making it worse for themselves.

Never before in my United-watching career have City been any better than rubbish, and whatever the immorality of their ill-gotten gains, competition is always welcome. So there was something really very satisfying in the way United were able to raise their game to keep the pretenders at arm's length – rather like Madrid did to us in the 2003 European Cup – restating beyond doubt the true order of things.

That order is underlined by the fact that for United, winning the tie had nothing whatsoever to do with winning a trophy that remains an insignificance; it was simply about making sure 33 became 34. Adding a year to City's proud tally is one of three imperatives that characterise each season, the others defence of the treble and ensuring Liverpool don't win the league. And in recent times – City this season, Liverpool last, and Arsenal in 2004 – whenever the situation has demanded a direct intervention, the players have responded with the vicious alacrity we're entitled to expect, so heartfelt appreciation for that, boys.

Although that's not why we love them – we love them because we have to – they do sometimes make it very easy indeed, and as we walk through the valley of the shadow of debt, we're grateful to spend a little while pretending that all's well with the world. It's been a while since I skipped my way to the car of a morning, even if the cynic in me was wondering whether United's approach to this derby – far more serious than in recent years – was prompted by instruction from above, aimed at quelling what has become widespread dissent.

Of course at half-time, it looked very different. Even though the City players were bound to be nervous, and even though Mancini was bound to organise them Italian-style, it seemed as though United's gameplan was to snatch the clinching goal in a last–20 minutes siege, folly in the extreme. Playing with neither urgency nor pace, City were allowed to gain in confidence when they should have been squashed, making for a nervier evening than was necessary.

The way they tore into them in the second half was far more like it, the frustration that they don't play that way all of the time. Although the standard of passing, shooting and the rest is understandably variable, aggression, composure, and commitment to attack should not be. After spending most of this season and last hanging around and passing it sideways, Carrick for once displayed his obvious ability when it really counted, and similarly Nani looked at last like he might understand his – no doubt he'll be replaced by Park on Sunday.

I wonder what Garry (with two 'r's) Cook made of it all. A worthy successor to Peter J Swales, Franny Lee, and friendly Dr Thaksin, he's never grown up from being the kid with tall stories that exists in every playground. You know the kind – plays for England schoolboys, dad's a black belt in karate, granddad discovered America.

His latest arrogation stated that City are poised to become "without doubt the biggest and best football club in the world", and that their trip to Wembley was a case of "not if but when, having beaten Man United yet again". The claim – made in New York's aptly-named Mad Hatter Pub – was later justified on the grounds that he didn't know that he was being filmed. Aha! Now I see! One can only be held to account for making outlandish claims when on *camera*. In that case I am the finest writer and finest looking man ever to walk the earth. And before anyone starts, I know United aren't exactly slow to crow either; the difference is that it's with good reason.

Craig Bellamy is another at the very top of his groundless gobshitery, clearly visible on telly shouting "you're finished, you're finished" to Rio Ferdinand during the second half. Whether or not he's right remains to be seen, but even if he is, at least Ferdinand managed to get started. Bellamy, on the other hand, has won nothing, come close to winning nothing, and built a reputation as a vile, cowardly thug with bad tattoos and peculiar posture. Perhaps that's why he's had so many clubs, though of course they're always handy for when you fancy whacking someone.

The Ferdinand incident came in the immediate aftermath of Bellamy being hit with a coin thrown by someone in the crowd. Although I'm not condoning that kind of thing, there is something delightfully karmic about it – Bellamy did, earlier in the season, make it his business to slap a fan already restrained by four stewards.

It's also worth pointing out how darling Craig's behaviour differed from that of Patrice Evra. In the first leg, Evra provoked City fans by retrieving the ball in order to take a throw-in, and was duly hit by a cigarette lighter. He reacted by looking with general disgust in the direction from which it came, and then got on with the game. In the second leg, Bellamy shouted abuse at United fans and was subsequently struck, so threw himself to the ground, bouncing up and stomping off once requisite attention had been sought, leaving someone else to take the corner. The corner was rubbish, United broke, and within seconds it was 1–0; well done Craigy.

Watching the game with a friend who had two sleeping children upstairs, that goal was the cue for the pair of us to scream without raising our voices – yes, I'm so happy I'll even paraphrase Bono. Then, after the winner, this was accompanied by a little jig, so that we missed the camera panning from the pained ecstasy etched into Rooney's face, to Tévez – who at full-time did not look remotely arsed – to van der Sar, to the City fans, a herd of what my Gran would call *farbrent farbisseners*.

Once the game was done, we were left peering round Terry Venables's goatee trying to watch those who'd remained in the ground to goad the away support. There was annoyance when this was interrupted by the post-match interviews, but only briefly

– Darren Fletcher's performance was of such magnificently wired intensity that it was lucky the kids were in bed.

And if that wasn't reward enough, it was quickly followed by the treat of Mancini, seemingly on the verge of tears. Showing how quickly he's contrated bluemoania, he snivelled his way through the lie that but for the "ten minutes" during which United scored twice (on 52 and 71), City were their equal. "Bitterly disappointed", said Jeff Stelling knowingly.

On the subject of bitterness, Blackburn's poor form has meant that we've not heard much from Sam Allardyce this season, but this week he saw fit to criticise Benny McCarthy for his disloyalty in leaving a club where's he's not getting picked, to join a better one, in a better location. This is the same Sam Allardyce who left Limerick for Preston, Preston for arch-rivals Blackpool, and Notts County for Bolton, publicly touting himself for the England job at every possible opportunity while he was at the Reebok. During that period, Allardyce was accused by the BBC of various other acts of gross loyalty, so there is no one better placed than he to demand it of his players.

The notion of loyalty in football is, in the main, nonsense. Players aren't employed by clubs as a favour that they're obliged to repay, rather are retained for as long as they're considered useful, and then shifted as soon as possible. So what grates isn't that players leave, but – provided they don't join a hated competitor – how they go about arranging their departure. Ronaldo, for example, didn't annoy anyone through his desire to play for Madrid, but by publicly pledging to stay and agitating for a move at the same tedious time.

Similarly, it was impossible to feel sympathy for David Sullivan, calling on karma to right the wrong of Eidur Gudyomtov preferring Spurs to Westairmfrewnfrew; why on earth wouldn't he? And the whinging is even harder to understand coming from someone who claimed to be a lifelong fan of one club, yet had no problem buying another.

It's funny that citers of karma almost always think that their misfortune is something going, rather than coming around –

it must be much less confusing if you're City, for whom fortune's a strictly one-way arrangement.

United 4 (Rooney 8, Rooney 82, Rooney 86, Rooney 90+2)
v Hull 0

United: van der Sar, Rafael, Ferdinand, Evans, Evra (Fábio 87), Park, Scholes (Gibson 72), Fletcher, Nani, Rooney, Owen (Berbatov 72). Unused subs: Kuszczak, Brown, Carrick, Valencia.

United 3 (Scholes 52, Carrick 71, Rooney 90+2) **v city 1**

United: van der Sar, Rafael (Brown 75), Ferdinand, Evans, Evra, Carrick, Scholes, Fletcher, Nani (Valencia 90), Rooney, Giggs. Unused subs: Kuszczak, Vidić, Park, Berbatov, Owen.

Arsenal away 31/01/10

How Gordon Brown must wish that he could call upon Wayne Rooney. Instead, he's had to make do with quantitative easing and Peter Mandelson, both far less adept at obscuring the truism that skint is skint is skint.

Though there's a limit even to Rooney's talents. Ten days ago, the worry was that a couple of respectable results might cause the resistance to lose focus, but it's now clear that the situation has escalated beyond that. But even though the second half at Arsenal was punctuated by loud anti-Glazer sentiment, if that doesn't translate to direct action – the only way of banishing them from our club – they'll continue laughing at us for evermore.

More interviews like the one given by David Gill last Sunday lunchtime won't do any harm, deceitfully spluttering his passive-aggressive way through a spot on 5 live. Despite questions less penetrating than a castrated fly, when not resorting to desperate escapes like "you'll have to ask the owners" – well we would if they could or would speak to us – and infantile retorts like "but you're not an accountant are you" – no, but we can count – he was demeaning us with a condescension that must be the only way of handling his very palpable guilt.

After once promising to be "behind the barricades" should the Glazer takeover succeed, the sorry lump of money-love was good enough to let us know that the demonstration planned for the Milan home game is "ridiculous". Though perhaps the biggest insult was his reference to United as a "family club". Family's club maybe, but family club? In the words of the late, great MC Ruff, officer me lord, you must be mad.

But let's humour him and run with it anyway. The roles of rich, senile old man and gormless kiddy-fiddling uncles are taken, Gill himself perfect as the interloper who's not actually a relation but manages to insinuate himself into the will nonetheless. And if Fergie's the aging patriarch who's wronged and righted everyone in his time, and the players the hired help, that only leaves the supporters; unwanted ginger stepkids who embarrass everyone, but won't keep quiet.

Anyway, to the relieving balm of the football. The famously lucid Paul Merson declared pre-match that "Arsenal could run riot", while Wenger commented that "we look always forward to it". Well perhaps they any more won't, after another demoralising hiding.

At least that's what it seemed like, based on the bits that I could see. No more than Arsenal and their plastic Hornbyites deserve, the Emirates is easily the worst of the new grounds, locating supporters as far from the pitch as possible, despite the promises made to the contrary when the idea was first sold. Fine, there are unobstructed sightlines, but you can get those on the telly; people go to games to be involved in the action, not to talk amongst themselves whilst it takes place somewhere in the distance.

No sooner had *The Wonder of You* finished – about as congruous at the football as a pink combine harvester embroidered with ermine – than United took over. Dominating possession and territory, they spent the first 20 minutes trying to break Arsenal down, Arsenal trying simply to break. Even though Arshavin had two half-chances in that period it would have been hard to worry had he scored, United's superiority such that they looked good for at least a couple of goals, as indeed they were.

The game's outstanding player in the first half was Nani, three consecutive performances of excellence illustrating what can be achieved via the complex strategy of picking a player consistently and in his position. After two years spent putting both the poo and the nani into poonani, when we saw him in a suit at Stamford Bridge, my dad speculated hopefully that perhaps he'd come from a job interview, and the majority of others, myself included, would have similarly rejoiced in his sale.

However this was always more an problem of personality rather than ability, his performances hampered by selfish, brainless indulgence on the ball and a demeanour of indignant entitlement off it. Now, in the opinion of no less a luminary than Micky Phelan, he looks like he might develop into "a United player", which it's nice to see he realises is about more than being picked to wear a United shirt. If he could just sort out his cheating and his hair, who knows – maybe one day he'll be a Red.

Given that so far this season, United have managed only a single league goal from over two hundred corners, the ability to score from the opposition's is very handy. And it's especially pleasing to see Arsenal undone in that way, a tactic some seem to think was patented by Wenger, rather than pioneered by Fergie.

Also worthy of note was its employment in the beating of a decent outfit, something Arsenal, for all their aesthetic demolitions of Charlton and West Ham, have rarely done. And whilst on the subject of Arsenal, I don't think I can remember a Wenger team so devoid of power and pace. For all the players with nice first touches, there was no one likely to beat a full-back on the outside, placing almost all the creative responsibility on Fábregas – a brilliant footballer, but one United have learnt to exclude from games between the sides.

Instrumental in doing so this time was what can only be hoped is now a settled midfield, that simple fact of greater importance than the personnel comprising it. Anderson's recent sulk means that Fletcher will be joined by either or both of Carrick and Scholes, the latter's passing deployed higher up the pitch at long last, where he remains perhaps the league's most intuitive unpicker of defences.

Of course it also helps if you have Wayne Rooney, devastating when given proper support. As well as his obvious technical skill, he has a natural stamina allows him to retain his top speed for longer than others, and married to a brain that sends him in the right direction, he's incredibly difficult to pick up. Long may he stroke his zits in triumphant post-match interviews.

But none of the above is to say the performance was perfect; United relaxed after the third goal when they should have been punishing Arsenal with four, five and six, though maybe they were under instructions not to decimate their confidence completely, as it'd be useful if they took points off Chelsea on Sunday.

Which brings us onto John Terry – as regular readers will know, a great friend of the blog. For the record, my contempt for Terry has never had anything to do with the fact that he captains a team with whom United compete, but is a consequence of the man we know him to be, advertised since the start of his career – repeatedly – through mannerism, deed and word.

Even now, accused of all sorts, after scoring the winner at Burnley he preferred to make a macho statement rather than trot sheepishly back for kick-off. Beating the club crest on his shirt in the direction of the Chelsea fans, what was he trying to say? I'm the man and that's what I'm about? This is what's important, and all that other stuff doesn't matter?

Then, in midweek, following Didier Drogba's goal at the KC, he turned to make a shushing gesture at the Hull fans who'd been taunting him. Maybe I'm just dense, but I'm struggling to fathom how an equaliser scored by a teammate renders cheating on your wife with your mate's ex irrelevant.

Terry's sense of the world may be warped in the extreme, but it's only a more heightened version of that shared by plenty of his fellow professionals: there is simply no transgression that cannot be eradicated either by money or on-pitch performance.

This particular misdemeanour is no more relevant to whether he should retain the England captaincy than any other, but predictably, there has been no shortage of people desperate to involve themselves in the non-debate. Sports Minister Gerry Sutcliffe, for example – as though anyone should or does care for his opinion – argued that the allegations necessarily compromised his position. How odd and yet typical for him to take a stand over consensual sex, yet remain silent over the rape of the national game and its clubs.

And then, of course, there's good old Harrance Redknapp, the very quintessence of honour, suddenly bemoaning the decadence of modern footballers who "do not come to me and ask me for advice". Strange indeed; were they to ever need a brief, there's surely no one whose recommendation counts for more.

Unsurprisingly, City have also found themselves powerless but to jump up and down in the hope that someone notices, three of their players wearing t-shirts with "Team Bridge" printed on them. Now I understand the idea of supporting a friend, but could they not just have told him? Do they not have his phone number? Attention-seeking twats one and all.

Astonishingly, the uproar has left Rio Ferdinand looking almost appealing, and in prime position to take over should Terry be stripped of the England captaincy – how very convenient. In fact the whole thing smells so suss that it can mean only one thing: John Terry, you've been merked.

Arsenal 1 v United 3 (Almunia o.g. 33, Rooney 37, Park 52)

United: van der Sar, Rafael, Brown, Evans, Evra, Fletcher, Scholes (Giggs 71), Carrick, Nani (Berbatov 89), Rooney, Park (Valencia 87). Unused subs: Kuszczak, de Laet, Gibson, Owen.

Portsmouth home 06/02/10

Villa away 10/02/10

Last Saturday was the 52nd anniversary of the Munich air crash. As I toasted the Babes with a large glass of malt (Highland Park 18 years, now that you ask), my girlfriend challenged me as to why I was remembering something that I couldn't remember.

In simple terms, it's fairly straightforward to transpose personal experience onto such intense embodiment of panache, youthfulness and strength, but that still doesn't quite capture the significance: for Reds of my generation, the Babes never died, because we know them only as the eternal heroes of tales that will last for eternity. Figments of our imagination and figures in our dreams, we grew up with the hope that someday they might come back so that, just once, we can watch them play.

This makes our relationship with them very different to that of our fathers. We can't possibly conceive the trauma of leaving for school glowing in the aftermath of an important victory, then coming home to find half the squad dead and the manager on the precipice. But it's woven into our psyche nonetheless, just like the events passed down through other aspects of our identity.

So to me, for example, the Babes are a motif in the same way as the slaves in Egypt, the Zionist pioneers and those who had the misfortune to be in Eastern Europe in the 30s and 40s. And like most momentous times, each is synonymous with song; The Spinners' memorial, *The Flowers of Manchester*, is one of the very first I can remember being touched by, though for years I thought United's outside-left was called David Peggalso.

The manner in which Matt Busby and Jimmy Murphy rebuilt the club in the aftermath of Munich makes its current predicament all the more mortifying, though the delight taken by followers of almost every other club is equally unsurprising. It isn't that we're seeking sympathy – emphatically we are not – and I understand that people are riled by our numbers, cockiness and success. But when the future of any club is jeopardised, it should be everybody's problem. However much I enjoyed the footballing aspect to Leeds' demise (and it was a lot), no set of supporters should have to suffer simply because the rules aren't strong enough to prevent idiotic or rapacious ruination.

Last Saturday's opponents Portsmouth are another case in point, not just of monetary ruin but of what Arsène Wenger calls financial doping – spending artificial wealth or borrowing heavily in pursuit of success. And rather like its athletics equivalent, it's not only dangerous but cheating.

Despite occupying bottom position, Portsmouth are nowhere near the worst side in the league. With the obvious exception of the unpleasant O'Hara, they're not a team of donkeys, generally passing the ball quite nicely before contriving to miss any ensuing chances; wobbling on the touchline like John Major's *Spitting Image* puppet, you could see why Avram Grant might urgently need a massage.

With Scholes and Giggs both rested, United lacked imagination in the middle of the pitch, only threatening-ish in the opening period. Nonetheless, a collection of goals always seemed likely, and a couple duly arrived before half-time, the first via a short corner – well oil beef oct!

Using a Danish stream running behind the action, I later encountered the oddity of watching a game live whilst knowing a goal was imminent, after glancing at the television to check another score at the same time United's updated. And what a goal it was, Berbatov's holding off some admittedly pathetic challenges to fire into the bottom corner with characteristically understated cool.

Even so, and despite an earlier scooped pass to Valencia that should also have resulted in a goal, there were still plenty of people criticising him afterwards. It's not quite a "what have the Romans ever done for us?" kind of deal, but neither is it far away – in a week's time, the game will be remembered for those two moments alone, what exactly is to discuss? The purest artist at Old Trafford since Verón, the prospect of witnessing not just the brilliant but the unforeseeable is something that should exist every time United play, and even when it ends in disappointment, the anticipation is worth the frustration every time.

A niggling injury and the success of the 4–3–3 formation meant that, as expected, Berbatov was back on the bench at Villa – thanks to Martin O'Neill, no longer one of the better aways. Considering themselves a half-decent outfit, it now costs 43 quid for a crap seat – far too much, even for one in the same row as prominent United characters Milky Milky, Napalm Death and Toni & Guy. The away allocation has been reduced too, and since last season – at O'Neill's behest – the away section moved from behind the goal, a petty attempt to gain an advantage that reflects badly on his team, as well as those suddenly and purportedly there to cheer them on.

It's impossible not to be needled by the loss of four points to Villa, particularly given how the games have unfolded. Crucial this time was the careless waste of the first 19 minutes, United only waking up after going behind. Immediately and thereafter, they played with urgency and intent, the lack of celebration for the equaliser at least indicating that they were suitably annoyed with themselves.

Down to ten men soon after, the slow start arguably cost United victory, though they remained the team more likely to prevail. Villa will have known they'd likely still be out-passed, and were legitimately wary of being caught on the break, but are nonetheless shamed for playing like a bunch of eunuchs.

United's chances of forcing the win probably ended with Giggs's injury – all we can do now is wait for Fergie to rush him back for Milan at home, in classic style. Although not playing particularly well, he was still the team's most astute finder of space, and replacing him with Park would at least have enabled the most likely scorer to stay nearest to the goal. Instead, Rooney went to left-midfield and Berbatov came on, receiving neither the service nor support he needed to make an impact, though I acknowledge that, on this occasion, it would've helped if he'd put himself about a bit more.

At least it looked strange seeing Rooney out wide, especially pleasing given that next week United play a Euro away. Let's hope they go to Milan and play with enterprise and courage – the Babes certainly would have done.

United 5 (Rooney 40, van den Borre o.g. 45, Hughes o.g. 59, Berbatov 62, Wilson o.g. 69) **v Portsmouth 0**

United: van der Sar, Neville, Brown, Evans, Evra, Valencia, Fletcher (Gibson 66), Carrick, Nani, Berbatov (Owen 66), Rooney (Diouf 66). Unused subs: Kuszczak, Fábio, de Laet, Park.

Villa 1 v United 1 (Collins o.g. 23)

United: van der Sar, Rafael, Brown, Evans, Evra, Carrick, Scholes (Valencia 46), Fletcher, Nani, Rooney, Giggs (Berbatov 74). Unused subs: Foster, Neville, Gibson, Park, Owen. Sent off: Nani.

Milan away 16/02/10

There was no shotgun shack or beautiful automobile, but racing along a gangway in front of the Milan fans celebrating United's third goal, arms flailing and shrieking like a braking train, I suddenly found myself asking a question made famous by Talking Heads: how did I get here? This was quickly followed by two more of my own: what the fuck am I doing, and how the fuck am I still alive? Sadly, I'll never know the answer to any of them; such is the price of the Champions League.

Repeated visits to the same cities impose no obligation to sightsee, entertainment sought instead in the twin pleasures of good food and good drink. If the former is easily found, the latter is perhaps too easily found, and raises problems of its own: how to measure the precise amount of red wine that will sustain a warming but not discombobulating buzz until after the post-match lock-in? Someone may have happened upon the formula, but it is most assuredly not me.

Losing my mates en route to the ground I somehow managed to wander into the curva sud, helpfully identifying my allegiance with a green and gold scarf. Exactly what happened next is unclear, the first half passing in something of a blur, and my only real memory is of being foxed by the perennially cunning interval into thinking the game was over.

Anyway, that turned out not to be the case, and I passed the second 45 standing on the aforementioned gangway, where I was offered no biscuits. Supervised by a steward and various home fans I befriended, people were surprisingly affable given my unrestrained goonery, though it would be disingenuous of me not to mention that by this time I'd detected a mysterious ache in the jaw area; my osso bucco must've been less tender than I thought.

Despite the recently-improved European record, there remain very few away wins against decent outfits during the Fergie years; two in Turin is about the sum, with nods towards Montpellier and Legia Warsaw if we're feeling exceptionally generous. Fergie trying to play tactics has probably been the major cause of the underachievement, and Tuesday was no exception, rejigging the midfield an entirely unnecessary measure. Even so, on this occasion the fault lay far more with the players, their play soft, tepid and sloppy, like a shit sandwich.

With so many culpable it'd be harsh to single out individuals, though Fergie felt no such indecision, subjecting Jonny Evans to a quite magnificent public *mapoleh* whilst everyone else enjoyed the equaliser. His malaise was hard to understand, given the composed way he handled last season's game at Inter, and it's tempting to put his indecision down to having to cover for the far less likeable and well-off-the-pace Ferdinand.

Although Scholes' equalising goal involved a significant element of luck, coming at the end of a quick and incisive move you'd expect him to finish, it wasn't quite the fluke suggested by Leonardo after the game. But it did provide United with the impetus to impose themselves in the proper manner thereafter, Fletcher dominating midfield with another display of aggression and intelligence.

But once again, the headlines went again to Wayne Rooney, hotter than Flasheart's pants and even more prolific, despatching two more of the headers that I criticised him for not scoring but a few weeks ago. Sulking through the first half and deciding that Nani was to blame after he was caught on his heels by a couple of pretty decent crosses, the second was a different story, his pace, strength and movement way too much for a very lame defence.

And as United left the San Siro in glorious victory, City were busy struggling to a draw against ten-man Stoke. After so many years of expert and perpetual failure, it was no shock to hear that they're contemplating a different sport, reportedly keen to invest in one of the new IPL cricket franchises. This also explained what Patrick Vieira was up to, getting in some early practice by taking aim at Glenn Whelan's middle stump.

The IPL is the very zenith of sport's defilement by business, taking place for no reason other than its ability to generate cash for people who already have plenty, at the expense of genuine competition. Thus it was fitting that the story broke the same week we heard of Premier League plans to allocate the final

Champions League spot via a playoff, a measure that would no doubt please the desperates at Wastelands.

On my very first Euro away – the 3-3 at Barcelona in 1999 – United fans were singing "we're here coz we won fuck all", poking fun at a tournament claiming to be for champions but also inviting participation from runners-up. This too was a ruse to make more money, but at least there was the consolation of a sporting angle – a competition featuring league winners alone could be sure only of having the best teams from the previous season. So despite the motivation, standards improved as a result, whereas admitting the seventh placed team would achieve quite the reverse.

Of course the proposal has been dressed up as serving the interests of fairness, but if that were really of interest then a salary cap, combined with a transfer cap, would be far more effective. This would allow teams to retain the advantages legitimately acquired over years of success and support, at the same time as preventing the distortion of the game by the likes of Chelsea, City, and, in a slightly different way, Real Madrid.

But that would restrict how much money could be made, which would never do; far better to protect the vested interests, regardless of what it means for the integrity of the competition. The NFL is a case in point: because an equal league makes more money, every step is taken to artificially arrange one. It may be less predictable, but winning the Superbowl is almost a rota, and there's not much glory in that.

The inspiration, both in sport and in life, might be the idea of being the best, but the challenge is fairly making the most of whatever abilities have been unfairly allocated. Otherwise, we're missing the point of Talking Heads' question.

Milan 2 v United 3 (Scholes 36, Rooney 66, Rooney 74)

United: van der Sar, Rafael, (Brown 90), Ferdinand, Evans, Evra, Carrick, Scholes, Fletcher, Nani (Valencia 64), Rooney, Park. Unused subs: Kuszczak, Neville, Gibson, Berbatov, Owen. Sent off: Carrick.

Everton away 20/02/10

West Ham home 23/02/10

There are three effects that make the demand curve slope upwards, and United tickets have segued their way through them all over the last twenty years. First an addiction, next a status maximiser, and then a giffen good – something you purchase because you've no choice.

But now, demand is plummeting faster than Alexander Lemming; in the week preceding the Westairmfrewnfrew game, the club desperately hawked seats to anyone they'd ever heard of, and at a discount; once upon a time a much-coveted privilege, now no better than a ruddy tulip.

It's not that tickets shouldn't be cheaper – of course they should be – but as a principle, not because of market forces. The apathy is both depressing and encouraging.

Tuesday's game followed a very disappointing effort at Everton the previous Saturday. Driving along the incongruously named Queens Drive and Maiden Lane an hour before kick-off, there was already some trepidation in the car amongst the less rational – despite decent recent history, this was a game United always lost when we were kids, and the clear, sunny conditions were also all wrong.

Walking towards the ground, the first local we encountered commented that we looked like United fans; good. With Liverpool supporters so repugnant, it's easy to forget that Evertonians aren't far removed, something given the old F5 by their behaviour on the way out of Wembley last season.

Despite sticking you down the side of the pitch, Goodison remains one of the better away trips, less plastic than most. Stood opposite the Swarfega hoarding that might be the world's most redundant advert, we were also directly behind one of the thoughtfully positioned pillars, and by the end, it would've done for there to be a few more.

The music played over the PA at football grounds nowadays is a typically soul-defiling mix of phoney pop and one-paced indy dronethems, but there was still a shock in store pre-match. If all it takes to get a record deal is a peculiar set of siblings, then, ladies and gentlemen, without further ado I give you Garil!

For a time it wasn't too bad seeing the older half lead the team out – local boy, loves the club, yadda yadda – but it's never really been enough. The captain of Manchester United must be scary, cool, or both, and a bumfluff moustache doesn't quite do it. In addition, Rafael needs games, not a rest, and after a display in Milan that was both chastening and encouraging, it's hard to see what's gained by leaving him out.

In the event, Neville was perhaps United's least bad defender, though the team actually started well and deservedly took the lead. The ease with which Valencia continually ran by Leighton Baines made a mockery of his claims to the England spot, suddenly vacant after the international retirement of Wayne Bridge. For his part, Bridge told us this week that he's "thought long and hard about his position". Wayne, I'm sure there have been a lot of long, hard...er...er...thoughts, plenty of them about position – maybe as many as 34.

Anyway, it looked briefly as though a relaxing afternoon was on the cards, before Bilyladetinov found a brilliant goal out of nowhere, and United never rediscovered their rhythm. As Jamie Redknapp has taught us, goals literally change games.

Although the subsidence was limp, credit to Everton, who are miles better than Villa, Spurs and City. Their midfielders manipulate ball and space intelligently, and they all ran backwards and forwards faster and in greater numbers that United. The second and third goals weren't exactly imminent when they arrived, except for the fact that they arrived, but both were likelier than one at the other end, the scoring combo of hair and tatt an additional whack in the goolies.

With United's victories of late arriving via 4–3–3, it might have helped for them to retain the same shape, though it was reasonable to compensate Berbatov for his consequential but undeserved omission. But even if he was the reason for the change in formation, he was also the team's most threatening attacker, and with Rooney quiet, subbing the next most likely scorer (after own goals) was never going to help, even if there was wisdom in the introduction of Scholes. The listless Carrick – a player who very rarely gets it did when others don't – would have been better told to sit at the side.

The midweek game was always likely to be easier. Westairmfrewnfrew's new owners, Sullivan and Gold, are the latest ideologues to come out in favour of a salary cap; I wonder if they'd be as keen on a limit levied on the earnings of pornographers. Tactfully alerting their players of an impending pay cut via the media, apparently these measures are necessary because the club are skinter than they thought. Well perhaps they should've done their due diligence properly then.

As far as the game went, United picked up the tempo well after a slow start. Lax in not knocking in a few more goals, at least the hiatus between the second and third allowed for a truly hilarious rendition of "we're gonna win fray toe". I'm not sure whether fray toe is a game or a condition, but I am sure that whenever United play a London club, I cringe with hope that I don't sound like they do.

With Tuesday's game being so winnable, on balance Fergie was probably right to rest a few players, hopefully ready to hand Villa what would be a very well-deserved beating on Sunday. This latest contribution to the Football League and FA's mortgage is costing me seventy sheets, for only the second-tier price-band – a mess they're sensibly exacerbating by bidding for a World Cup Haiti's got more chance of hosting. Still, I suppose funding incompetence beats funding avarice.

Everton 3 v United 1 (Berbatov 16)

United: van der Sar, Neville, Brown, Evans, Evra, Valencia (Owen 81), Fletcher, Carrick, Park (Obertan 66), Rooney, Berbatov (Scholes 66). Unused subs: Foster, Vidić, Rafael, Gibson.

United 3 (Rooney 38, Rooney 55, Owen 80) **v West Ham 0**

United: Foster, Neville, Brown, Vidić, Evra, Valencia, Gibson, Scholes, Anderson (Park 19), Berbatov (Owen 78), Rooney (Diouf 78). Unused subs: Kuszczak, Rafael, Evans, Fletcher.

Villa Wembley 28/02/10

For more than fifteen years, philosophers have been vexed by what it was that Meatloaf wouldn't do for love, but the reality is that he was deluding himself; if he'd really been serious, then "that" wouldn't exist. Such is the price of true love, such is its distinction from self-interested love.

Many United supporters now find themselves in a similar quandary. Unfairly, perhaps, given the countless ruined relationships, lost jobs, missed parties and decimated bank accounts, but nonetheless "that" time has arrived.

This week, a consortium of wealthy Reds announced an intention to buy the club, the ultimate aim to transfer ownership to the fans. But seeking to buy United and actually buying United are two very different things; if, as expected, the Glazers refuse to sell, they'll need to be forced. With no other financial squeezes obviously available, it's likely that the only way of getting rid is to boycott Old Trafford.

Although we've been here before, circumstances are different now, the motivation effect rather than principle. In 2005, people stopped going because they refused to let the Glazers buy United with their money, but in 2010 it'll be to secure the future of the club for eternity. And the beauty is that it wouldn't entail any missed games – if no one renewed, they'd be gone faster than their foreskins.

Enter the Red Knights. Lame moniker, admittedly, but should they pull this off, they'll deserve to join Sir Gawain, Sir Galahad and the rest of the boys, and no doubt Guinevere and the Lady of the Lake will be eager to show their gratitude too.

As ever, in that context football hardly seems relevant, except, of course, that of course it is, and what an excellent week it's been. February felt too early in the season to want City to win, but then, with a little help from our old friend Hilario, they beat Chelsea and suddenly it very much wasn't. How absolutely delicious; even when they get it right, they get it wrong. D'oh!

At least they were compensated the following day with Dennis Tueart's memorable triumph in the BBC's best ever League Cup goal competition, the award presented before this season's final. I do very much hope he enjoyed the game, even if it wasn't as good as the 1986 Full Members Cup classic.

Neither did the pre-match fun end there, the teams revealed alternately amidst soldiers and flags, Villa's announcer compounding the embarrassment by handing each player a nickname that'd shame even the thickest dartist. However the house resident soon outdid him, variously reminding us of the teams, match and score; but another example of how officialdom considers us all morons.

Although we'd all like every game to be watched by screaming nutters, the United end was as low-key as you'd expect, plenty leaving before the trophy was presented. If nothing else, though, it was worth staying to see it lifted by the wonderful Patrice Evra, well on the way to becoming a genuine Red legend. The best left-back in the world according to most unbiased judges, since very early in his time at United he's spoken with passion and eloquence about who and what the club represents, usually in magically unhinged style. Most recently, he revealed tacit support for the anti-Glazer protest, until now a position stated only by Cantona and Solskjaer; high-class company indeed.

With Rooney not starting the game, a lot of creative responsibility rested with Berbatov, typically disregarding the pre-match pomposity by standing out of line during the introductions. Maverick non-conformity or self-indulgent apathy depending on your bent, he had a splendid game, as did Owen in the time that he was on. Say what you like about his first touch, hamstrings, height, vision, scouseness and character – and I really do mean that – but he's always scored in big games, and if he stood near Berbatov for any length of time, he'd get a whole lot more.

The football in the first half was actually quite decent and by far the best I've seen at Wembley, 70 quid lower tier seats way better than the 90 quidders I've been mugged for in the past. Although Villa started well, United gradually took over, with Carrick showing some uncharacteristic but very pleasing aggression, and Park and Fletcher also influential.

Things were duller after the interval, the second 45 spent waiting for United to score, which they duly did, Valencia now far better at locating Rooney's head than his hair. It was just unfortunate that when he repeated the trick moments later, his NBF hit the post, saving Villa fans ten painful minutes of certain defeat.

The major controversy of the game was Phil Dowd's decision not to send Vidić off for his foul on Agbonlahor, another player with a nickname on the back of his shirt; until his unique hat-trick of impregnations, he was plain old Gabby Agbonla. You do, though, have to wonder what Vidić thought he was doing – after getting away with an initial shirt-pull that prompted a slip and a check, a block rather than a tackle would probably have sufficed and even if not, Agbonlahor wouldn't necessarily have beaten Kuszczak.

Although it was the referee rather than the law found wanting here, the provision that stipulates dismissal on the denial of a goalscoring opportunity could do with a tweak. It was instituted to stop the "professional foul" – a situation in which a defender prevents a likely goal without attempting to play the ball – but punishes those who make legitimate efforts at prevention more harshly than is fair. If the referees could be trusted, it'd make far more sense to show a red card only if there was no genuine attempt at a tackle, or if the attempt was reckless – *Cunningham*, not *Caldwell* – with no chance of success.

To finish this week, three very special winners of the Barry Ferguson, honoured for remarkably hypocritical disses, but of oh so deserving causes. The first goes to Jamie O'Hara for decking Michael Brown, the second to Craig Bellamy for his bravura slating of "JT", and, finally, Rafael Benítez for his criticism of Sam Allardyce.

So, despite myself, congratulations to all; it just goes to show, hatred isn't blind. Neither should love be.

United 2 (Owen 13, Rooney 74) **v Villa 1**

United: Kuszczak, Rafael (Neville 65), Vidić, Evans, Evra, Valencia, Fletcher, Carrick, Park (Gibson 83), Owen (Rooney), Berbatov. Unused subs: Foster, Scholes, Diouf.

Wolves away 06/03/10

Milan home 10/03/10

The older we get the less frequently life puts us in the kind of peculiar situations that make it worth the trouble, one of the many reasons going to the game endures when we think we've experienced it all. Thus I forced myself to be thankful when, relaxed in a cubicle at Molineux Asda, suddenly I was being stared at by a packed gallery of fat, sweaty men, now-open door tantalisingly out of reach.

Not having been to Wolves for a while, I'd forgotten what a dive the ground is, and not in a good way, stands down the sides a totally unnecessary distance from the pitch. Neither they, nor the tactic of stationing away fans along the entire length of one of them, do anything for the atmosphere, though when the home fans are satisfied with karaoke *Hi Ho Silver Lining*, I suppose it's a losing battle.

Unfortunately the players no longer emerge from separate tunnels, Premier League self-importance dictating a slow march that I guarantee is practised in far fewer gardens and bedrooms than was the slightly inclined jog. But slow marches it is, preceding a "respect handshake" that ought really to be a fist bump. Then, trying to succeed where the crowd failed, the Wolves players indulged in a very long very useless very unintimidating huddle whilst Mick McLobanovski looked on, mind pregnant with innovation.

Because United were so poor in the first half, there could be no possible ambiguity as to whether or not a half-time rollocking was required, although the players were also hindered by the selection. In the absence of Rooney, it was risky to rest Fletcher, the midfielder most likely to run beyond Berbatov and the team's next best player. And as a consequence of his absence, we were subjected to yet another useless effort from The DFG, unable to spell his name let alone lace his boots.

On what should have been a 4–4–2 day, Owen's injury was felt immediately; he isn't the standard required, but not to notice how sharp he looked at Wembley would be to ignore it on purpose, and chances are he'd have found at least one vital goal in the run-in that fuck knows where it'll come from now. Though should

United manage any more trophies, he'll look very smart stood clapping in his suit.

Things improved with the introduction of Diouf, offering more of a presence up front despite delivering the most inept cameo since the heady days of Forlán. But like Forlán, he appears to have a knack either for making things happen or for stumbling across them as they happen to be taking place – if he could learn some composure, he might yet turn out to be useful.

Which brings us nicely on to all-round hero Paul Aaron Scholes. A goal that's certain before it arrives is a rare occurrence, but the extended moment of expectation, excitement and relief duly began as soon as he picked up the loose ball. No matter that it was a difficult chance; that it would be stuck away in consummate fashion was never in doubt, Craddock and his girly name put on their arses for good measure.

The importance of winning a fourth consecutive and record 19th title meant that I'd hardly thought about Milan until after Wolves, though it was hard to see them containing the brilliantly elusive Rooney well enough to win, playing Machida to Thiago Silva's Thiago Silva. Predictably, Fletcher was also to the fore, elbows sharper than Florian and Loiseau combined, whilst Park – far more convincing as a midfielder than a winger – ran like a beserker, and is a genuine alternative to Carrick in that position. Thus his goal was well-deserved, coming from close enough range so that even he could muster the force to get the ball over the line, though there was of course a typical stumble in the process.

Most happily of all, the defence looked close to regaining its old solidity. This was despite the presence of Gary Neville, his selection explained by the ever-insightful Mark Lawrenson on the basis that "he brings lots and lots of pragmatism". In a newspaper interview last weekend, Neville referred to the hype that surrounds football as "noise and fluff" – pretty much all he contributes nowadays – but credit to him on this occasion. Similarly, Ferdinand and Vidić played with authority and calm too, the former even winning the kind of crucial but dangerous header his dashing good looks usually insist he bottle.

United also deserve praise for their approach. In the two seasons since Quieroz left, the attacking emphasis that underpinned the 1999 European Cup win has returned, even if Fergie's half-time snap that "we don't defend a lead" was not a small bit rich – though not as rich as his comments after the game, when he said:

"Paul Ince unfortunately went to play for Liverpool so they weren't exactly throwing garlands at him when he came back but normally they always appreciate the players who have had great careers at this club."

So who might *"they"* be, then? *"They"* who caned him in their autobiography and publicly referred to him as a "big-time Charlie"? It must also be *"they"* who were responsible for the various briefings against Beckham, van Nistelrooy and the rest, as well as the countless negative European performances that are suddenly such an affront; damn them!

If the tedium of the Beckham angle ruined the pre-match anticipation, it was well worth it for his post-match scarf-wearing. Of course it's not going to make the Glazers sell, and presumably we'll have to suffer the annoyance of anything green and gold suddenly termed "David Beckham-style", but job done nonetheless. And at least he diverted attention from Fergie's dark coat, light trousers faux pas, unusual for someone who usually looks bang on when in official gear.

The fuss over Beckham unfortunately distracted people from footage Capturing the Glazers pointing and laughing at protesting fans; yes, *they* were suggesting that *other people* look stupid. Whilst the contempt with which they regard supporters has never been in doubt, this was clearly a pre-meditated gesture, and it tells you that they're rattled; the door is well and truly open, and they know we're watching.

Wolves 0 v United 1 (Scholes 72)

United: van der Sar, Brown (Neville 46), Ferdinand, Vidić, Evra, Scholes, Gibson (Diouf 62), Carrick, Valencia, Berbatov, Nani (Park 73).
Unused Subs: Foster, Rafael, Fletcher, Obertan.

United 4 (Rooney 13, Rooney 46, Park 59, Fletcher 88) **v Milan 0**

United: van der Sar, Neville (Rafael 66), Ferdinand, Vidić, Evra, Valencia, Park, Scholes (Gibson 73), Fletcher, Nani, Rooney (Berbatov 66).
Unused subs: Kuszczak, Evans, Obertan, Diouf.

Fulham home 14/03/10

It's a beautiful sunny day high up in the French Alps, and the very first of my snowboarding career. The air is pure, the mountains spectacular, life good: what better to do than pace around a chalet in wet thermal underwear, listening to the United game down the telephone?

Though I appreciated the refuge from the aggressive slopes that had already left me a battered mess, and could also hide behind the excuse of work, the only legitimate explanation for such ridiculous behaviour is the obsession times addiction equation that identifies the truly sick.

As anyone who's traipsed around foreign cities in search of football can testify, unfortunately – and to the vociferous chagrin of any travelling companions – there's no other choice. Quite simply, the guilt at not seeing a game and the fear of what might be missed insist that no hassle is too great; I need United, and cling to the fanciful notion that somehow they need me.

And never is it easy. On this occasion I'd left open the possibility of getting on with my life, but predictably, as kick-off approached the panic set in, and I frantically flapped to the pub. Contingency kyboshed with the leaving of my laptop on the plane, when it turned out to be closed, the only option was to return to the chalet. But even this was a hassle, the receptionist claiming a busyness so insanely intense that spending a few seconds passing me a spare key was impossible, necessitating a rather sharp conversation in order that she be convinced of the urgency of my need. It's a long old while since I've listened to United on the radio, and it was almost a treat, the chance to imagine your own pictures offset by the anticlimax of celebrating a goal once it's too late, the lonely, stilted shout one of relief rather than ecstasy.

Although a win against Fulham is no longer as predictable as it once was, I'll refrain from joining the list of ignoramii to patronise Terry Tibbs Hodgson, an obviously astute coach. Beaten by them twice in two seasons, United are more aware of this than most, and even though their performances were more craven than the Cottage itself, Fulham played very well in both games.

In the event, the points were secured fairly easily, though the first goal took a while to turn up. Created by Nani's intelligent pass – not words I ever supposed I'd type – whilst less effective when not deployed on the right, he's gradually learning to trust his left foot. The chance was, of course, greedily snaffled by Rooney, and though he's attracted the majority of the plaudits, it's noticeable that almost every goal he scores is celebrated with a run and a point in the direction of whoever's made it easy for him; his finishing has been superb, but the service has been even better.

United's recent attacking verve has left Fergie with something of a selection problem ahead of the Liverpool game, Park, Nani and Valencia all demanding inclusion and Giggs close to fitness. And Berbatov is playing well too, earning extra points for the haughty way he handed Murphy his shirt at full-time, declining the one offered in return.

In theory having so many in form is a reason to be cheerful, but the reality is that I'm annoyed in advance at the multiple team changes that will no doubt ensue at a time when there's little margin for error, largely a consequence of the selfsame indulgence. It's all part of the fabled but untrue cliché, invented and perpetuated by Fergie, that United never get going until Christmas, as though taking half the season off is some kind of lovable quirk, rather than an insulting excuse for an unacceptable lack of intensity.

Thus as the season nears its end, that United are still in with a chance of winning the league is a significant piece of fortune. We can only trust that they'll win when they have to, which last time around was the very finest route to success, tantalising Liverpool with the prospect of the title before cruelly destroying their hopes in the most gloriously demoralising fashion.

United suffered similar disappointment in 1992, but where they returned to win the league a year later, the Scousers have opted to indulge in the self-pity that has made their city famous. No one has embraced this tendency with greater alacrity than Rafael Benítez, whinging and comfort eating in equal measure. This week, he informed us that "everyone knows you can have a bad season every now and again", but actually it'd make more sense to replace "bad" with "good".

The facht is that Liverpool's run in 2008/09 was anomalous, exceptional form from their two decent players combining with eightiesesque luck and decisions to make them appear better than they were; now, they're simply performing to their level. That said, they've continued to enjoy the benefits of favourable judgments from the relevant bodies regardless of the evidence, the delightful Steven Gerrard in particular. Though it would be churlish to entirely castigate his latest infraction – you wait ages for Michael Brown to get a slap and then two come along at once – the decision not to suspend him is certainly worth another look.

Apparently, Gerrard can't be punished for a forearm smash worthy of Johnny Cougar because the referee saw the incident and dealt with it at the time. If that really is so – he witnessed an assault and felt it merited nothing more than a talking to – then he should be granted a few weeks off too, for a quite appalling decision. But of course that's not really what happened; rather, he's unwilling to admit his mistake, so instead it all gets swept under the forehead. Gerrard may be a Phil Collins fan, but it appears that where he's concerned, seeing isn't believing.

Let's hope that retribution is handed out on the pitch instead, via humiliating and richly deserved defeat; how not to be addicted to that?

United 3 (Rooney 46, Rooney 84, Berbatov 89) **v Fulham 0**

United: van der Sar, Neville 6 (Fábio 87), Ferdinand, Vidić, Evra, Valencia (Park 73), Carrick, Fletcher, Nani, Berbatov, Rooney. Unused subs: Kuszczak, Gill, C Evans, Obertan, Diouf.

Liverpool home 21/03/10

There are very few things that would be enjoyable if you did them all the time; pleasure is partly relative. Thus Wizzard didn't really want it to be Christmas every day any more than the ecstasy debutant wants to be high all of the time; the triumph of the instinctive over the realistic and the moralising is transient, or as Freud might put it, the ego and superego generally balance the id.

At the most basic level, the id is the part of the psyche that football tickles, resulting in intense, disordered impulses that it's incredibly hard to restrain. So beating Liverpool is one of those very few things that can never become routine, as it's neither impractical nor overindulgent.

Unfortunately, this time there was no hiding, and also no last minute steal, but disposing of the scousers in such routine, perfunctory fashion is, though a different joy still a joy, and marvellously soul destroying in its own unique way. Even after United fell behind, thanks largely to the kind of gruesome defending that has spooked them all season, there was no panic. Rather, the players composed themselves, and though not at their best, made it very clear that their superiority would translate into number of goals required to win the game.

That isn't to say the id went entirely uncurbed, critical superego reminding us that the performance was impeded by the players' ego. In not pursuing a third goal against opponents as impotent as their flavescent shorts suggested, undue caution overpowered gluttonous gratification, to almost catastrophic avail.

Slowing the pace allowed Liverpool to feel comfortable in the game, intimating that it was close. Sit on a one-goal lead against any side, and a law of averages chance will almost certainly turn up, which you can only hope won't be taken. Of course, when it does, and is ineptly missed by little Violet Elizabeth Torres, it becomes a decent idea, but the tactic was still ill-calculated and cowardly.

The first twenty minutes actually featured some decent football from both sides, United hindered by Carrick – who had another miserable day – giving away possession as freely as one might a deferred public spending cut. Luckily Fletcher was alongside him, who, despite not playing as well as he can, was still easily the game's most influential performer. Responsible for providing the winning goal, that he should be one of United's best crossers (and a decent dead-ball option) is unsurprising; for a top professional, it's really not a difficult skill if you can be bothered to practice. Unlike a pass, it needn't be pinpoint, just delivered into the right area for an onrushing teammate to make it appear judged to perfection.

On Sunday that was Park, far more useful in a midfield three than instead of a proper winger, his energy partially compensating for a lack of wit in the absence of Giggs, Scholes and Berbatov. A game against a decent team would require at least one of them, but at the moment it should be at Carrick's expense.

After another good display from Valenthia, now seems a suitable time to say that although he was crap at the start of the season, he's actually a lot better than I thought. Most attacking players I've seen arrive at United have either done it immediately or not at all, but he's a rare exception, reminiscent in style of Andrei Kanchelskis and showing increasing ability to improvise.

With everyone fit and in form, the team is now more able to handle changes in personnel and formation, also when Fergie is at his most dangerous. At the start of the season, all that was required was to leave the team alone for the first few games; if he had, title 19 would be almost won. Though of course – in another cliché he's disseminated in an attempt to turn the incompetent into the endearing – "we always make it hard for ourselves". Whoever wins the league will deserve it by virtue of having the most points and therefore being the best team over the course of the season, but it would be embarrassing to see either of these Arsenal or Chelsea sides dance around with our trophy. Well, figuratively speaking – in reality I would obviously protect my eyes from any such images.

Winning the European Cup is an altogether tougher proposition, and I'd be far more confident of beating Munich were the first leg at home. Playing away first allows the opposition to start on the front foot, also giving them the threat and potential trump card of an unmatchable second leg away goal, as well half an hour more to get one in the event of extra time. But then the concept is flawed in the first place; one goal is worth the same as any other, and the demand for artificial entertainment oughtn't to supersede that essential ex-truism.

Any further progress in Europe takes United closer to a game with Barca, a rematch it's easy to be bold about this far in advance. In the meantime, it'll be enjoyable to watch them put a hurting on Arsenal whilst picturing Darren Fletcher lanking round the Bernabeu with Xavi in the crook of one arm, Iniesta in the other.

But there's a fair way to go before then – for now, I'm having nightmares about Arjen Robben degrading Gary Neville. I wonder how Freud would explain that.

United 2 (Rooney 12, Park 60) **v Liverpool 1**

United: van der Sar, Neville, Ferdinand, Vidić, Evra, Carrick, Fletcher, Valencia, Park (Scholes 87), Nani (Giggs 79), Rooney. Unused subs: Kuszczak, Rafael, Evans, Obertan, Berbatov.

Bolton away 27/03/10

Munich away 30/03/10

"It's like when you put your head to the grass. You can hear it growing. You can hear the insects, bzzz".

This, apparently, is the sound of the calm before the storm – well, at least according to Stansfield, Gary Oldman's character in Léon and one of my desert island movie psychos.

But it's only because he's a psycho that he's capable of enjoying the moment; most normal people can't wait for it to be over, either on account of the tension or the overwhelming desire to know how things will pan out. And with games against Chelsea and Bayern coming up, we've reached precisely that part of the season.

The week began at Bolton, a place that will never fail to amaze with its tableau of awkward faces contorted in one-way hatred, a bit like me suddenly deciding that I don't like John Steinbeck; surely Blackburn and Burnley would be more receptive? Outside the ground, the song of choice was "we love you Glazer", the response of "you love your sister" cheap and crude, but then so are many of the very best things.

The Reebok really is a monstrosity, what a space station made by Ikea might look like. In an imaginative attempt at giving it some character, four cheap banners have been stationed in the home end, one next to the other, reading "Owen Coyle's Superwhite Army", "Owen Coyle's Superwhite Army", "Owen Coyle's Superwhite Army" and "Owen Coyle's Superwhite Army" respectively. And on a drape of canvas either side hang two very weird pictures of Lee, the kind of thing you might find on the duvet of a teenage girl in South Korea...I imagine...or I don't. Whatever, you know what I mean.

It does, though, have the kind of section that all grounds should, full of coatless young scriffs paying little and behaving badly. That same area also played temporary host to a small group of United equivalents, the majority of them winning the game of British Bulldog required to get into the away end.

Prior to the game – in addition to lying about Rooney's availability – Fergie slipped in yet another of his patented advance excuses, asserting that "everyone will drop points" so as to justify any ceded by United. And sure enough, for an hour that looked possible, Bolton missing enough decent chances to have Gary Neville jumping and stamping like Yosemite Sam on a period. The best of them were wasted by Elmander, though Cohen missed a good one too. "Roll on Shabbes, you shouldn't roll on Shabbes", the United end didn't chorus.

That said, United looked dangerous every time they upped the tempo, and the passing was generally sharp. When the first goal came, it was no surprise to see that man Own Goals on the scoresheet once more, and never injured nor suspended, he'll need to step up again in the absence of Rooney.

Following the half-time treat of bagpipe *Yankee Doodle*, United were more fluid in the second period, Berbatov mixing his usual Nietzschean artistry with some Millish utilitarianism, two deceptively tricky chances dispatched with both style and economy of effort. This made it a very decent day, thanks also to Arsène Wenger's misplaced arrogance in believing that Arsenal not only have a chance of winning the European Cup, but are good enough to rest players in its pursuit.

But the way this season has gone, it was little surprise that a good run of form ended as abruptly as it did. On top of that, my flight was delayed, meaning there was not even enough time in Munich to visit Adidas Originals, and I also discovered that those responsible for the price of my flight increasing twice in the time it took me to pay were grown men with Premier League badges sewn onto their away strips. And yes, of course they'd purchased speedy boarding too.

Greeted at the airport by a stench of effluence that foreshadowed United's performance, I made quickly for the train into the city. Relaxing in the knowledge that when abroad, other people's inanities are just noise, it instead turned out that almost every person in the vicinity wanted a conversation. Note to self: must look more menacing in future.

Talking of future menaces, it seems very much as though the Green and Gold movement is meandering towards death, its sad futility perfectly encapsulated on the way to the game. Carriages full of people singing their hatred for the owners, clad in megastore-purchased sportswear, a shout of "if you really fucking hate them, don't renew" elicited no response save a veiled threat.

In the two months since the bond document stimulated a fresh surge of anger, the only call to action has been a request to sign a petition – hardly likely to intimidate the Glazers into selling. This absence of dynamic and decisive wartime leadership has been crucial, those with perceived locus unwilling to call for a boycott of Old Trafford. Similarly reticent to state any remotely controversial position, the iron is cooling rapidly, people too focused on the football to care about ownership.

The Allianz Arena is, I suppose, what the Reebok is attempting to be, an artificial eyesore that's also tackily impressive. In terms of the actual game, United were so poor that it's hard to provide much analysis beyond that one simple fact; whether they sat back after scoring or were simply hamstrung by shit-the-bed passing is impossible to say.

So obvious was the malaise that Fergie was uncharacteristically bold and proactive in changing things early, any benefit in introducing Berbatov and Valencia negated by incorrect withdrawals. Though Carrick was easily the most deserving, taking off Park as well left Fletcher with far too much to do in a midfield already overrun, and Bayern's winner was entirely merited.

With Rooney's injury an additional heel to the solar plexus, the responsibility now lies with Fergie to reconfigure the team in his absence, making sure that Berbatov receives the necessary support. Frighteningly, two 1–0 wins will suffice, not exactly the anticipated storm; we can only hope that he likes Beethoven.

Bolton 0 v United 4 (Samuel o.g. 38, Berbatov 69, Berbatov 78, Gibson 82)

United: van der Sar, Neville, Vidić, Evans, Evra, Fletcher (Gibson 80), Scholes (Carrick 74), Valencia, Giggs (Macheda 84), Nani, Berbatov. Unused subs: Kuszczak, Rafael, de Laet, Park.

Bayern Munich 2 v United 1 (Rooney 2)

United: van der Sar, Neville, Ferdinand, Vidić, Evra, Nani (Giggs 82), Fletcher, Carrick (Valencia 70), Scholes, Park (Berbatov 70), Rooney. Unused subs: Kuszczak, Rafael, Evans, Gibson.

Chelsea home 03/04/10

Munich home 07/04/10

Towards the end of Wednesday's game against Bayern Munich, ITV commentator Peter Drury informed viewers that United's centre-backs had been "penetrated twice". And I must say, I know how they feel, consecutive defeats annihilating an entire season in a single week of gratuitous incompetence.

There are few moments, however dark or light, that aren't enhanced by recollecting United's status as league champions. Now, for the first time in nearly four years, the prospect of being without it is within genuine contemplation, life suddenly less bearable, less good, or both. Who knows when we may next feel that surge of delight?

No doubt some will wonder what I'm bitching about, characterising me as the archetypal spoilt United fan, but it's a matter of relative expectation; or as Marx might put it, from each according to his ability, each according to his need. United have no right to succeed, but we absolutely have the right to demand it of them.

Disappointment is intensified by the belief that United lost to teams they could and should have beaten. Chelsea think they played well, United certainly played badly, yet the margin of victory was still slim. Similarly, elimination from Europe was equally unnecessary, though at least avoids a conclusion identical to last season's, and for less money. But regardless of the outcome of a cup competition, claiming United as Europe's best team – in either 08/09 or 09/10 – would require a case of redeye so severe as to make an addiction to bong hits and Mace the only possible explanation.

Luckily, we have the Glazer circumstance to divert our attention from on-pitch matters, easily trumping the sting of any defeat – a bit like remembering that there's always somebody worse off than yourself, then discovering that that somebody is also you. And for extra punishment I now have to write about it, or maybe this is just therapy. I hope that at least you're all wearing Melfian short skirts.

If the loss to Munich brought frustration tinged with invigoration, after Chelsea, the overriding emotion was one of anger. Quite simply, the players had absolutely no business performing as badly as they did, but, once again, they were – as my gran would've said – "velly poohwer". Presented with an opportunity not only to make the decisive move in the championship race, but also to guarantee that one of the most unpleasant squads ever assembled would be remembered only as the team that always finished second to United, they underperformed to quite startling extent. Each one of them deserves a pants-down, over-the-edge-of-the-couch smacked bottom.

And none merit it more than Fergie; that I grimaced at United's line-up almost as much as at Chelsea's tells you just how inappropriate it was, almost entirely devoid of the speed required to underpin its indisputable guile. Against a fit, mobile side, fielding all the *alti kackers* together was stupidity of the very basest variety, inviting them to outrun and thus outplay us for 45 whole minutes.

Lethargic of thought and movement, though it was obvious which team had played an intense game in midweek, it shouldn't have been. The sums players are paid might not affect how long and hard their bodies can go, but the increased energy they found in the second half suggests that they were either lazy or badly prepared; my money is on the latter.

Of course, the absence of Rooney didn't help, who though not winning games alone, remains the team's focal point. It's clear to all but those who matter that Berbatov is wasted up front on his own, as is the stupidity of effectively playing without a striker, but sure enough that was how the starting eleven set up, the predictable tardiness of Macheda's introduction intensifying the irk.

Throughout the season United have relied on strong second half showings to rescue frittered firsts, and unable to quite manage it this time, were deservedly punished. Events were a little reminiscent of Arsenal's win at Old Trafford in spring 1998, though Chelsea are nowhere near as good as they were, so hope is not yet lost.

Nonetheless, when the sole solace is in Joe Cole's expanding bald patch, things are not great.

And neither was the referee, United on the wrong end of some fairly clear-cut decisions to match those in the game between the sides at Stamford Bridge, when they were also not good enough to make them irrelevant. Whilst on this occasion the glaring errors were evenly distributed, the chronology benefitted Chelsea; the obvious penalty denied them would never have arisen had United been awarded theirs, and likewise, though Macheda's classic Italian finish ought probably to have been disallowed, it came nowhere near repairing the damage caused by Drogba's offside goal.

Onto the Munich second leg, and a selection that brought tacit acknowledgement of what a mess had been made of the previous two attempts. Pleasing and galling at the same time, so also was the tempo of United's game; whatever the outcome, there ought never to be a doubt that the players will step to, and for 41 minutes they did exactly that, with predictable results.

But within a further ten they had ruined it all, careless defending ceding Bayern the initiative, compounded by Rafael's sending off. Given the quality of the opposing wingers, it was inevitable that he would be forced into the commission of at least one yellow card offence during the 90 minutes, making a booking for retaliation inexcusable. Though we'd all like to kick Mark van Bommel, hard, and more than once, as soon as he did, his sending off became unfathomably inevitable, that it was for another non-emergency adding to the stupidity. And in beseeching the referee to take action, the behaviour of Ribery was all that might be expected of a man whose name sounds like some kind of bizarre sexual practice.

Still, at least we were permitted a little satisfaction first, Valencia making an example of Badstuber – an even worse full-back than extinguisher of cigarettes – and Nani enjoying his most effective game by far, transplanted brain now fully operational. Hell, even the selection of The DFG worked out; he may possess only a single discernible ability, but you can't argue that it's a goodun.

Sadly, after picking an excellent team, Fergie responded badly to every subsequent challenge; leaving Rooney on far too long, replacing him with an unfit defender, inviting pressure with no out-ball, not bringing on Berbatov immediately after going behind in the tie, not replacing Gibson who contributed nothing in the second half. Though United missed chances to score a fourth, the abovementioned ineptitudes made Bayern's goal a matter of time, and the ease with which they shut United down subsequently was both impressive and demoralising, not to mention a little sore.

United 1 (Macheda 81) **v Chelsea 2**

United: van der Sar, Neville, Vidić, Ferdinand, Evra, Valencia, Fletcher (Gibson 86), Scholes (Nani 72), Giggs, Park (Macheda 71), Berbatov.
Unused subs: Kuszczak, Rafael, de Laet, Carrick.

United 3 (Gibson 3, Nani 7, Nani 41) **v Bayern Munich 2**

United: van der Sar, Rafael, Vidić, Ferdinand, Evra, Valencia, Fletcher, Gibson (Giggs 80), Carrick (Berbatov 80), Valencia, Rooney (O'Shea 55), Nani.
Unused subs: Kuszczak, Evans, Scholes, Macheda.
Sent off: Rafael.

Blackburn away 11/04/10

There was a time when people thought that the Earth was at the centre of the universe, orbited by all other objects. Even when this was disproved by Copernicus and Galileo, it was some time before anyone paid attention – entrenched beliefs are hard to shift. But finally, it became impossible for people to query what they could see with their own telescopically-enhanced eyes, and theory became fact.

So when United, first against Chelsea and then Bayern Munich, supplied incontrovertible evidence that zest and pace are essential components of any cohesive football team, it was fair to assume that even stubborn old geocentric Fergie would accept what he once knew, but of course he did not. Though in the press conference prior to the Blackburn game we were warned of his likely selection, there remained the hope that it was yet another lie, but sadly it was not; the oldies were back, and unsurprisingly, they soiled themselves.

Still, at least Fletcher will be well refreshed for his summer holiday and O'Shea closer to what passes for match-fitness in time for his. Meanwhile Rafael – so outstanding in Europe – was once again left out, enabling the return of Gary Neville and the ball flipped aimlessly around the corner. It's not even as though his youthfulness gives him the monopoly on stupidity, Neville's needless handball ceding the free kick from which Munich scored their first-leg equaliser, but he was recalled nonetheless, no doubt on account of his "experience". Or in other words, Fergie was worried about Blackburn. Yes, Blackburn.

Blackburn really is a horrible place, cold even when it's hot, dark even when it's light. Walking towards the ground, a carload of fat goths in football shirts momentarily distracted from the team selection, but 20 minutes later we'd all remembered again, watching Nani and Macheda perform the worst shooting practice in living memory whilst Berbatov wandered around artistically, understandably reticent to bother himself with such frivolities.

At least this time he was given a striking partner, though very much the wrong one. For now, Macheda's limited all-round game makes him no more than a very handy sub; stationing him on the shoulder of the last man to use the pace he doesn't have was never likely to work, and the ball wasn't in the box enough for him to exploit his knack for finding space.

Thus what ensued was a dull first half, United dominating possession but with less edge than a velvet-covered circle. Fortunately, events were livened up by a midget in a Blackburn away shirt, posturing in front of the United end for reasons best known to himself. And the thrills continued through the break, during which we enjoyed Blackburn's goal of the season competition, the shortlist comprised largely of tap-ins, headers and scuffs.

The second 45 brought little improvement. It did, however, provide a vehicle for Sam Allardyce to prove once and for all that he can coach more than the traditional English stereotype – not only are his team remarkably well-schooled in the art of time wasting but his ball boys too, continental sophisticates all. And how unfeasibly apt that a personality of such divine magnitude and humility be sponsored by a company called Zeus, the man himself no doubt flattered by the association.

As the half sputtered on, it became increasingly obvious that no one was going to score, the flow broken both by the concession of needless free kicks and knobs in the away end hilariously hanging on to the ball after yet another crap shot. Chasing a game, even on the occasions that the required goals don't arrive, you expect United to make it look like they might, but bereft of ideas and enthusiasm, the anticipated onslaught never materialised.

A sizeable contingent of United's following seemed to blame this stolidity on Berbatov, though he stood out as the first half's sole piece of sweetcorn before succumbing to his surroundings in the second. As with Tévez last season, it's been painful watching Fergie slowly eviscerate his confidence, and if there was a chance of getting in a replacement anywhere near as good, then it'd probably be time to let him flourish elsewhere.

Again, the absence of Rooney didn't help; if Cantona was the footballing equivalent of Lebowski's rug that tied the room together, then Rooney is the room itself, without whom furniture is irrelevant. This is the direct consequence of a squad replete with complementary players, men able to facilitate but not instigate, the lack of individual inspiration leading to dropped points when the collective underperforms.

Thus the players were reduced to appealing for imaginary penalties, the support waiting for the inevitable and depressing defiance of *Forever and Ever*. At least we're almost out of our misery, though the lameness with which the title has been surrendered will annoy for evermore.

For this the fault lies mainly with Fergie, making nowhere near the best use of the squad afforded – or not afforded him, and reduced to desperately and transparently challenging Bolton to prove they're not "an easy game". And now that's failed, we're relying on flaky Tottenham and plain useless Liverpool to help us out, on the basis that United can be relied upon to also help themselves, which of course they cannot.

So it was that by late Sunday afternoon, the club's official website bore the headline: "Boss rues poor decisions". "I should jolly well say so," is a broad and less profane approximation of what I thought, but it turned out that Fergie was criticising his players, rather than admitting culpability for the errors that have made such a mess of everything. The earth may be at the centre of our universe, but for Fergie there'll only ever be one thing at the centre of his.

Blackburn 0 v United 0

United: van der Sar, Neville, Ferdinand, Vidić, O'Shea (Evra 79), Valencia, Scholes, Giggs (Gibson 57), Nani, Berbatov, Macheda (Park 65).
Unused subs: Kuszczak, Evans, Fletcher, Obertan.

city away 17/04/10

United, eh? Bloody hell! All the pseudory in the world couldn't do justice to the pandemonium of yet another last-minute winner against City, though of course I'll have a go. United, eh? Bloody hell!

Once again, every claim, every threat, every promise, demolished in a devastating swish of red, or as Wordsworth would have it, "sweet is the lore which nature brings". And though approaching it from the opposite perspective, Shakespeare knew it too, teaching Macbeth the same lesson; you can't subvert how things are meant to be, and should you try, the inevitable restoration of what's right and proper is going to sting. A very lot.

On the way to the game, I concede that I was looking forward to the end of the slog through another season – as ever, I expected United to win, but with a weariness that reflected the last couple of weeks. And this was piqued upon reading Fergie's comments that this was the first time he'd faced City when they could "achieve something"; there is no need whatsoever to encourage the kind of sickeningly empty self-congratulation that would follow their triumph in The Battle For Fourth Place TM.

Though chronologically speaking, this next bit belongs at the end, there's quite simply no way I can wait to discuss the lunacy that has just this second come to my attention. In the summer, City are to release a feature film – shot, would you believe on "cinema quality 'Red' camera", and – and get a load of this: it will recount "one of the greatest years in any club's history".

Now the Football League was founded in 1888, making this the 122nd campaign, taking wartime breaks into account. So should City snide their way into finishing fourth, that'll make 366 better seasons that have definitely been had – in England alone, and without even mentioning teams who've finished lower but won a cup, nor those who've not watched in horror as their local rivals cavort in the insane ecstasy of threepeating last-minute wins.

But that's City for you, and as you'd expect, there's more – loads, loads more. Apparently, "*Blue Moon Rising* reinforces Manchester

City's standing as the most fascinating story in the world of football". That's right, not only are City the single best thing that the game has to offer, but this is acknowledged by all as a generally accepted truth – though I suppose if you're talking screwball tragicomedy, fair enough.

And no doubt the star of the show will be Garry Cook, everyone's favourite encapsulation of inadequacy. Walking through the carpark before the game, it was no surprise whatsoever to note that not only does he drive a jeep, but one with a personalised plate to match; why on earth would the people behind *not* want to know his initials?

The City of Manchester stadium is one of those perpetually windy places that you never want to be. Desolate, empty and humourless, it's only a matter of time before a tumbleweed blows across the pitch, though presumably it'll now be excused as a respectful concession to cinematic grammar.

Meanwhile, in the stands, a smattering of Bayern Munich garnished the usual baby blue, luxuriating in the excuse provided by United's elimination from Europe. And if that wasn't intimidating enough, we then got to see the City fans dancing to Blue Moon once again, a truly fearsome sight – think epileptic wino tramp.

Shortly after, the players turned up, the sight of Rooney breaking off from the line-up in chest-out, arms-wide bound something of a comfort. It turned out that he was patently unfit, indicating quite how ridiculous it was to leave him on for so long against Bayern, almost ten days earlier. Nonetheless, he was still more use than Tévez and Bellamy combined, the top answer in Family Fortunes' "Things you might chain to a stag" survey.

Mancini's selection of a one-paced two-man in-adequate midfield allowed United to dominate possession in the first half so that City's wingers and strikers were prevented from participating in proceedings. They were, however, disciplined at the back, defending deep and in numbers, United not quite slick enough to pull them apart and faltering around the edge of the box, fortunately missing the chances that did arrive; well done them. Chief culprit was Giggs, suffering his way through a frustrating performance cast in his own inimitable style. Taking up good positions and seemingly just about to do something good, each opportunity was quickly ruined with weak flicks and bad passing, supplemented by a diet of horrendous set-pieces.

After the break came more of the same, United in control but offering no concerted threat. When Mancini replaced Johnson with Vieira, it appeared as though he'd settled for a point, but the arrival of Wright-Phillips and Ireland soon after opened things up, and City actually had the better of the final ten minutes, before the extra space afforded United told, St. Paul's brilliant header securing a deserved win.

What happened next is unclear. Joy, hope, hatred, love, relief, aggression, bodies cascading, tumbling, bouncing, and spinning... phew...for a minute there I lost myself.

Having remained in row three for precisely such an occasion, I came to in the middle of a scrum over the lip of the stand, feasting on the ire that the stewards were unable to hide. Making sure to get in a few blind-side digs, one particularly elegant and ladylike type was physically struggling to contain herself, twitching away to the merriment of one and all, though I'm not sure why anyone was that bothered – *Superbia in Proelio* after all.

It was at this point – in fact deep in the throws of "a passion for football rarely seen on the silver screen" – that I realised I'd forgotten to take in the reactions of the bitters, and what a scene it was: heads in hands, hands on tops of heads, hands behind heads, hands over eyes; iconic, filmic, and poster perfect.

At the final whistle, time taken to befriend the vanquished still inside the ground was punished by missing the barehanded dung-throwing outside. Instead, we were forced to cavort behind a locked gate until permitted to leave, making up for lost time by running through the streets dispensing free lifestyle coaching as we went. Then, a weeklong struggle not to manipulate every conversation to be about the game, fists clenching themselves at irregular intervals. United, eh? Bloody hell!

city 0 v United 1 (Scholes 90+3)

United: van der Sar, Neville, Vidić, Evans, Evra, Fletcher , Scholes, Gibson (Nani 59), Valencia (Obertan 80), Rooney (Berbatov 74), Giggs. Unused subs: Kuszczak, Rafael, O'Shea, Carrick.

Spurs home 24/04/10

Whether it's King Lear, Jules Winfield or Reginald Cousins, the storytelling canon is replete with parables of redemption, however improbable. And there are few more so than the tale of Luís Carlos Almeida da Cunha – or da complete Cunha, as he used to be known.

Given his full name, Nani may sound like a character dreamed up by Gabriel García Márquez, and though a whole lot less sympathetic, he's experienced fluctuations in fortune just like Buendía and co. But now, though his face remains as eminently slappable as ever it was, things are going his way to the extent that a virtue can even be made out of the attitude that is so vexing, the beauty of his arrogance a total absence of nerves.

In much the same way there was never any doubt he'd score his penalty in Moscow, through on Gomes last Saturday – or Goams as my Cambridge-educated girlfriend called him – the outcome was equally sure. If the mind has no sense of its own fallibility, then it need never feel apprehension, at least until replaced by the kind of self-aware insouciance that wound up hindering Ronaldo's performances.

Anyway, thanks to United's wins over City and Tottenham, and Tottenham's defeat of Chelsea, there's still a chance – albeit an outside one – that the league might be retained. And having experienced both in recent weeks, I can confirm that hope beats despair, whatever Brian Stimpson might think.

Unfortunate circumstance dictated that the Spurs game be watched in the pub, an option selected only in very precise circumstances, or when in dire need. Fortunately it was pretty much empty save the oddity of a pair of Mancunian brothers, one red, the other blue – and more curiously still, not after the vaguely explicable Andy-and-Steve-McDonald-older-City-younger-United fashion. On the one hand I felt I should chastise the elder for allowing his family to become thus contaminated, on the other, how not to respect the definitive piece of sibling bullying?

Considering there was something at stake for both sides, the game began in fairly dull style. Amusingly, Spurs decided to retain possession through sideways and backwards passing as though they were good enough to pick their moment, instead losing the ball immediately they attempted anything remotely difficult. Particularly culpable was Huddlestone, very keen on displaying ability he wishes he had, and less use than a rock on which people gather to share body warmth. Best that he stick to poncing around London nightclubs with his top off.

After half an hour or so, United began to apply requisite pressure, Spurs suddenly unable to hang with them. Noticeable as ever was the difference Rafael made to the attacking variety, not just in his crossing and comfort on the ball, but with his eye for a pass. Also handy is his willingness to keep running after playing it, turning up unmarked in places you wouldn't expect to find a right-back. He may get caught out of position every now and again, but so what? He plays for United, thus is entitled to expect others to cover for him.

In that light, it's aggravating to hear that Gary Neville has scabbed himself another contract. Though he's a decent enough emergency option, he clearly won't be reserved solely for those occasions, thereby obstructing Rafael's development and also that of the team. Given the presence in the squad of Brown and O'Shea too, along with Fergie's love of spreading the games around, there'll also be a reduction in the opportunities available to Fábio and Smalling.

United played ok in the second half, though bouts of on-pitch vomiting from Nani and Evra suggested that someone had snuck a copy of *Scroatie McBoogerballs* into the dressing room. But despite the inconvenient side-effect, its artistic inspiration was undeniable, those two instrumental in the eventual win.

A full-back with the skills of a winger, in his time at United Evra has neither scored nor created enough goals – a harsh criticism, given his outstanding contribution to the cause, but a fair one nonetheless – so it was pleasing to see him win the penalty that led to the first goal, following on from his assist for last week's derby winner. And immediately Giggs despatched it, Spurs did their best to concede another, desperate to alleviate the pressure of competition.

Thus they were rather fortunate to equalise, a rare attack defended badly and resulting in an undeserved goal from a corner. Redknapp's introduction of Gudyomtov also made a difference, and it was strange, particularly given the tactics, that he hadn't been selected to start the game. Equally, it was surprising that he replaced Defoe, who though an overrated piece of egotism, has the pace that would have made him a better outlet than Pavlyuchenko.

Before the game, the relative quality of the substitute benches was a slight concern, Macheda United's lone game-changing option. Though he's not exactly impressed, there was surely more sense in having Diouf available – and if he's injured, Joshua King, even – than both Brown and O'Shea, to say nothing of Owen Hargreaves, part Jeremy Bentham, part Bernie Lomax.

Chasing a winner, United were either running out of ideas or patiently refusing to panic when it arrived. Tottenham, though, were convinced by its imminence, United's scoring of late goals a self-perpetuating prophecy that preys on tired legs and minds after they've spent an hour and a half chasing the ball.

So, it's over to Liverpool who, Benítez said this week "lack offensive players". Now I'm not sure about that, but as we've learnt with Nani, things you like about people can sometimes be things you dislike. Therefore let us hope they show their fabled ability to scrape undeserved results against superior opposition and take a point or three off Chelsea. But that's where it'd end – some things are beyond redemption.

United 3 (Giggs pen 58, Nani 81, Giggs pen 86) **v Tottenham 1**

United: Foster, Rafael (Macheda 79), Vidić, Evans, Evra (O'Shea 57), Fletcher, Scholes, Giggs, Valencia (Carrick 59), Berbatov, Nani. Unused subs: Kuszczak, Brown, Hargreaves, Gibson.

Sunderland away 01/05/10

When Nabokov said "caress the detail, the divine detail", he may have been advising other writers, but at the same time he was making a transferable point. Both pleasure and distress are characterised not via general and unspecific feelings, but by precise aspects that explain to us why we feel as we do.

Thus on the way to Sunderland, what was winding me up wasn't the prospect of United no longer being champions, but the way Steven Gerrard's errant backpass had suddenly woven itself into both Liverpool and Chelsea's history, a quirk of circumstance giving colour and uniqueness to something I was desperate be nondescript.

So before the game, excitement at seeing United play was for once as much reliant on the cognitive as the instinctive. It wasn't that anyone expected anything more from Liverpool – not because they're untrustworthy, although they are, but because they're rubbish. And not rubbish like a scrunched up piece of paper is rubbish, but rubbish in the way of a sewer full of festering flesh, food and effluence. United deserve shames and hand-wagglings galore for losing to such an inept bunch of malcoordinated nonentities.

If only we'd been able to teleport George Courtney over to Anfield from nearby Spennymoor. A bedrock of Liverpool's 80s success, having him reprise his uncanny knack for rescuing them one last time would have been well worth the trade-off of being permanently accessible to your parents and significant other.

Luckily the locals were on hand to lighten the mood, and what a joy it was to watch them do runway for us, smizing, finding the light and modelling H2T; Miss Jay Alexander would've been in raptures.

Kicking it first were a group of street cornered youths lunching on White Lightning and dispensing casual racism in the direction of any passing Asians. Closer to the ground, the crowd was a particularly dense shade of fat and a testament to many lifetimes of lipid abuse, the exception a value pack of badly tanned, haphazardly made-up, improbably thin young girls, apparently there to publicise Sunderland's backing of England's World Cup bid. I'm absolutely certain FIFA is taking note.

Other characters worthy of record included girls in evening dresses, girls with blue snooker chalk on their noses, many men sporting the muscles-tattoos-no hair combo, and several of the fastest eaters in the world. Though perhaps the weirdest sight was a middle-aged lady in a specially prepared half-Sunderland half-Chelsea shirt. Matching her half-and-half yellow-black hair and equally hybrid male-female appearance, perhaps it was some kind of fancy dress theme, and certainly showed a quite remarkable level of effort, along with an equally astounding ability to care about other people's business.

A friend of mine who watches Sunderland has often commented that, ideally, he'd do so in grounds empty save for him and a few selected family members, and it was easy to see why. And this position was only given further credence as the afternoon progressed, chants of Chelsea accompanied by strains of *You'll Never Walk Alone* – smalltime to the very nth degree.

Hearing the teams, there was an enjoyable symmetry in discovering that both brothers Ferdinand adorned their respective benches, the younger model – in the loosest possible sense – not even brought on when Mensah went off, despite his formidable IQ.

Anyway, United performed very well given the circumstances, playing with authority and composure in producing the kind of getting it done show that has served them so well over the years. If only they'd have mustered the same at Blackburn.

For the second time in three weeks, the game was run by Paul Scholes, who after a ropey period has relocated his genius. Though feted as a man of the people for his play the game, get showered, go home attitude, how many of us can actually say that given such extravagant gifts, success and exchequer, we would behave in similarly unassuming fashion?

Scholes was ably supported by those around him, Vidić, Evans, Rooney and Evra playing particularly well, Giggs hampered by his own carelessness and the ineptitude of the slug-ish O'Shea behind him. Meanwhile, Nani was a constant threat, and has even added tackling back to his repertoire of excellence, meriting specific praise for the hard time he gave the horrible Richardson, now banished to left-back along with the number 10 shirt he so obliviously requested.

Meanwhile, after an excellent afternoon against Spurs, Berbatov seized a bout of terrible form from nowhere, displaying the sort of Sadim effect that makes it seem like losses need cutting. It's harsh to reduce two years of being messed around to two instances, but the late chances missed against Chelsea and Blackburn were his moments and he failed to embrace them, the second in particular showing a lack of composure that is the last thing you'd expect of him.

Even as the game wound down and United settled for a single goal, Sunderland could muster no real threat, the roond mooth excitement that produces such a peculiar pitch restricted to a few isolated moments. To protect the lead, Fergie brought Ferdinand into the tall yet rubbish in the air role, one usually filled (and then devoured) by O'Shea. And with a minute to go, on came none other than Owen Hargreaves, hair and beard exactly as you'd expect from someone who's had a gap year or two. I wonder what a United shirt would look like in tie-dye.

Talking of the idle, it would be remiss not to mention that the 90 minutes were punctuated by bursts of police trotting up the stairs in the away end to no apparent purpose, unless there was some sort of skivers' social club at the top of the stand. The amount of money spent on unnecessary boy dem is a gravy train that really ought to be explained: this season, for example, the only hint of trouble I've seen was initiated by the police and, at a game where the away allocation was cut to 1,700, you have to wonder what they can possibly have expected to unfold.

Thus it was with particular resentment that I read Greater Manchester Police's statement this week, responding to criticism of how they've treated those voicing displeasure with the Glazers. Apparently, it "has a policy of allowing peaceful protest to take place". How very good of it! Gosh, what even-handed liberalism! But how about this: actually, it shouldn't matter a single iota what the GMP's "policy" is. The right to protest peacefully is enshrined in law, not within the gift of some jumped-up police chief, and anyone who suggests different can caress my divine detail.

Sunderland 0 v United 1 (Nani 28)

United: van der Sar, O'Shea, Vidić, Evans, Evra, Nani (Hargreaves 90), Scholes, Fletcher (Ferdinand 87), Giggs, Berbatov (Carrick 71), Rooney.
Unused subs: Foster, Brown, Park, Macheda.

Stoke home 09/05/10

One of the fringe benefits of following a football team is the way it enables the charting of life, anchoring unrelated but parallel experiences in time and place. But to every up there's a down: when things go badly, definitive connotations are unavoidably forced upon feelings that deserve to stand alone, happy times contaminated with disappointment.

So it is that my girlfriend's 30th birthday celebrations will be forever entwined with ceding the title, though if you will get yourself born in the second week of May and then succumb to a Unitedaholic, you've only yourself to blame. And spare a thought too for poor Greenwich Village, no longer just a trigger for simple associations of Bob Dylan, Jimi Hendrix and some good nights out, but now inextricably linked to the same unfortunate event.

At least the time difference meant that it was all over and done with by lunchtime, meaning less time to wait in grim expectation – though only in the US could live sport be shown on delay, so as to squeeze in a few more commercials – and more time to dull the pain with celebratory refreshments.

The game itself was an exercise in tolerance. Though I stationed myself in such a position as to ensure that there was no way I could see the screen showing Chelsea, however much the urge to ogle at unpleasantness challenged me, it was impossible to insulate myself from the hell yeah whooping and hollering emanating from its direction. Luckily, my attention was diverted by the replica-clad girl on the next table, who taught me that "Berbatov is like, so awful", amongst other gobbets of wisdom.

In terms of leagues not won, the sting of losing this time was relatively minor, a slap in the face rather than a boot in the balls. The run-in of 1992 served as an inoculation against all subsequent on-pitch failures, though I admit to my seduction by the prospect of setting a new record for pretty leagues all in a row, at the same time as overtaking Liverpool's total tally. And, of course, by the selfish desire to sell souvenir books, though despite drawing on my bar mitzvah and losing on my 18th birthday, in the main United have won when I've needed them to the most, the titles won in each of my three years as a student particularly appreciated.

That isn't to say it's enjoyable being bested by a squad including Terry, Lampard, Cole, other Cole, Drogba and Ballack, because it isn't, and that's without even getting started on Abramovich. But even in that context, Chelsea mean very little, the artificial nature of their success and support according them no real significance. Nonetheless, having accumulated the most points, they've been unarguably the best team, so, through gritted soul, congratulations to them.

As for United, they had a better season than I thought they might have done, though not as good a season as they should have done. Whenever a league is narrowly lost, there'll be specific moments that it's easy to blame, most obviously the arse-end of the decisions in both games against Chelsea. But though they did make a crucial difference, there were also plenty of opportunities to render them irrelevant, in particular the failure to cash in on an easy run of games either side of the New Year, and it's frustrating that the title was surrendered without forcing the winners to produce something exceptional.

And in the same way Fergie has been credited with dragging his men to titles in the past, this time he made nowhere near the best use of the resources available to him. Or in other words, had I been in charge, United would still be champions, and most likely preparing for another European final. I say this not because I rate myself as a manager, though clearly I do, but because the errors in selection and tactics have been of such obvious and glaring nature. As it happens, similar ones were also made last season and to a lesser degree the one before, but Ronaldo and occasionally Tévez were on-hand to mask them, whereas this time round, there was no such security.

In public at least, Fergie has been keen to voice satisfaction with how things went, despite a third consecutive year of decline. Earlier in the week, he confided that "I look into my own management and the rest of the staff. Did I always make the right team selections with the appropriate tactics? Do we have a strong enough squad?", the implication being that he did and we do.

Any such notions are, of course, utterly fatuous. There exist exceptionally clear cases of incorrect selection – Liverpool away and Chelsea at home, for example – and also of tactics, both Bayern games springing immediately to mind. And incontrovertible proof that the squad isn't strong enough was provided by the season-ruining effect of Rooney's brief absence.

In reality, the likelihood is that Fergie is cognisant of at least this third aspect, his ability to do something about it dependent on whom he can sell and how much more debt the Glazer credit card can wear. Foster will certainly be for the off, as will Berbatov if a buyer can be found. Carrick, too, is done, his contribution fading in line with the team – unsurprising from a player who reflects rather than inflects – and at long industrious last, Park has also fallen out of favour.

In terms of additions, more than anything, an attacking midfielder of genuine class is required – there are plenty of good players at United, but not enough brilliant ones. This season, when the whole team has clicked, they've played very well, but lacking has been individuals able to conjure victory when things are going badly.

Accordingly, the end of the season doesn't merit the kind of pontificating crescendo I had planned, thus, all that remains to say is thanks for reading, thanks for your comments, and next year in Jerusalem!

United 4 (Fletcher 31, Giggs 38, Higginbotham o.g. 54, Park 84) **v Stoke 0**

United: van der Sar, Neville, Ferdinand, Vidić, Evra, Nani, Fletcher, Scholes (Gibson 62), Giggs, Berbatov (Macheda 62), Rooney (Park 77). Unused subs: Foster, O'Shea, Evans, Carrick.